The Entrapment Defense
in North Carolina

The Entrapment Defense in North Carolina

John Rubin

2001

UNC
SCHOOL OF
GOVERNMENT

ESTABLISHED IN 1931, the Institute of Government provides training, advisory, and research services to public officials and others interested in the operation of state and local government in North Carolina. A part of The University of North Carolina at Chapel Hill, the Institute also administers the university's Master of Public Administration Program.

Each year approximately 14,000 city, county, and state officials attend one or more of the 230 classes, seminars, and conferences offered by the Institute. Faculty members annually publish up to fifty books, bulletins, and other reference works related to state and local government. Each day that the General Assembly is in session, the Institute's *Daily Bulletin*, available in print and electronically, reports on the day's activities for members of the legislature and others who need to follow the course of legislation. An extensive Web site (http://ncinfo.iog.unc.edu/) provides access to publications and faculty research, course listings, program and service information, and links to other useful sites related to government.

Support for the Institute's operations comes from various sources, including state appropriations, local government membership dues, private contributions, publication sales, and service contracts. For more information about the Institute, visit the Web site or call (919) 966-5381.

Michael R. Smith, DIRECTOR
Thomas H. Thornburg, ASSOCIATE DIRECTOR FOR PROGRAMS
Patricia A. Langelier, ASSOCIATE DIRECTOR FOR PLANNING AND OPERATIONS
Ann C. Simpson, ASSOCIATE DIRECTOR FOR DEVELOPMENT

FACULTY

Gregory S. Allison
Stephen Allred
David N. Ammons
A. Fleming Bell, II
Maureen M. Berner
Frayda S. Bluestein
Mark F. Botts
Phillip Boyle
Joan G. Brannon
Anita R. Brown-Graham
William A. Campbell
Stevens H. Clarke
Anne S. Davidson
Anne M. Dellinger

James C. Drennan
Richard D. Ducker
Robert L. Farb
Joseph S. Ferrell
Susan Leigh Flinspach
Kimberly Martin Grantham
Milton S. Heath, Jr.
Cheryl Daniels Howell
Joseph E. Hunt
Kurt J. Jenne
Robert P. Joyce
David M. Lawrence
Charles D. Liner
Ben F. Loeb, Jr.

Janet Mason
Laurie L. Mesibov
Jill D. Moore
David W. Owens
William C. Rivenbark
John Rubin
John L. Saxon
Jessica Smith
John B. Stephens
A. John Vogt
Richard Whisnant
Gordon P. Whitaker
Warren Jake Wicker

© 2001 School of Government
The University of North Carolina at Chapel Hill

⊖ This publication is printed on permanent, acid-free paper in compliance with the North Carolina General Statutes.

Printed in the United States of America

Book and cover design by Robby Poore

21 20 19 18 17   5 6 7 8 9

ISBN-13: 978-1-56011-388-1
ISBN-10: 1-56011-388-X

Contents

Preface vii

1 History of the Entrapment Defense 1

2 Rules of Entrapment 7

§ 2.1 Effect of Defense 9

§ 2.2 The Subjective and Objective Tests 11

§ 2.3 What Constitutes Inducement? 13

(a) Generally 13

(b) Inducement Not Found 14

(c) Inducement Found 16

§ 2.4 Who Are Government Agents? 18

(a) Generally 18

(b) Private Persons 19

(c) Unwitting Intermediaries 21

§ 2.5 What Constitutes Predisposition? 23

(a) Generally 23

(b) Relevant Factors 24

(c) Timing of Government Contact 28

3 Related Defenses 31

§ 3.1 Want of Element 33

(a) Generally 33

(b) Crimes Involving Lack of Consent 34

(c) Conspiracy 35

(d) Stolen Goods 36

(e) Drug Offenses 37

§ 3.2 Reliance Defenses 38

(a) Entrapment by Estoppel 38

(b) Public Authority 39

(c) Innocent Intent 40

§ 3.3 OUTRAGEOUS GOVERNMENT CONDUCT 40

    (a)   Generally 40

    (b)   Procedure for Raising 42

§ 3.4 SENTENCING ENTRAPMENT 44

4   Procedural Issues 47

§ 4.1 DISCLOSURE OF INFORMANTS' IDENTITIES 49

§ 4.2 SEVERANCE OF CO-DEFENDANTS 51

§ 4.3 INCONSISTENT DEFENSES 52

    (a)   Generally 52

    (b)   A Rule and Some Exceptions 53

    (c)   Illustration 57

    (d)   A Simpler Approach? 57

5   Evidentiary Issues 59

§ 5.1 PRIOR BAD ACTS 61

    (a)   Generally 61

    (b)   Relevancy Restrictions 63

    (c)   Hearsay Restrictions 66

    (d)   Prior Good Acts 68

§ 5.2 REPUTATION EVIDENCE 69

§ 5.3 CONVERSATIONS WITH OFFICERS AND INFORMANTS 72

§ 5.4 EXPERT TESTIMONY 72

6   Burdens and Instructions 75

§ 6.1 BURDEN OF PLEADING 77

§ 6.2 BURDENS OF PROOF 77

    (a)   Persuading the Jury 78

    (b)   Obtaining Jury Instructions 79

    (c)   Avoiding or Obtaining Nonsuit 82

§ 6.3 JURY INSTRUCTIONS 83

    (a)   Giving of Instructions 83

    (b)   Wording of Instructions 84

Table of Cases 89

Table of Statutes and Rules 95

References 97

Subject Index 101

Preface

This is the second in a series of books I plan to write on North Carolina criminal law defenses. The first, on the law of self-defense and related defenses, was published by the Institute of Government in 1996. This one, on the entrapment defense, is intended to serve a similar purpose: to provide a comprehensive resource, specific to North Carolina, for judges, lawyers, and others who work in the criminal justice system.

Why write about criminal defenses? Certainly practitioners do not work with them nearly as often as they do other aspects of criminal law, such as the elements of criminal offenses. Because they do not work with defenses regularly, however, practitioners also are not nearly as well versed in their operation. My hope is that, when situations do arise in which a close understanding of entrapment becomes necessary, this volume will provide answers to, or at least ways of thinking about, the most important issues to be addressed.

Chapter 1 of the book sets the stage for the discussion of North Carolina's rules of entrapment. It reviews the federal origins of the defense and the continuing importance of federal law in the development of the defense.

Chapters 2 and 3 discuss the substantive rules of entrapment and related defenses in North Carolina. Chapter 2 describes in detail the test for establishing entrapment in North Carolina, which requires that the defendant show both that the government induced him or her to commit the offense and that he or she was not predisposed to commit the offense. Chapter 3 discusses related defenses, ones sometimes raised along with or in lieu of an entrapment defense. For example, if a law enforcement officer or other person sets a trap for the defendant in a way that undermines an essential element of the offense charged, the defendant is entitled to acquittal regardless of whether he or she satisfies the requirements of entrapment.

The remaining chapters discuss questions that may arise in the trial of cases involving an entrapment defense. Chapter 4 discusses procedural issues—for example, the rather confusing rules on whether a defendant may deny having committed the offense alleged and still claim entrapment. Chapter 5 discusses common evidentiary issues that may arise at trial, including the admissibility of evidence of the defendant's prior crimes or other wrongs. Chapter 6, the closing chapter, analyzes the respective burdens of proof borne by the prosecution and defendant. It also offers guidance regarding the wording of jury instructions on entrapment should the defendant produce sufficient evidence to warrant submitting the defense to the jury.

For those interested in reading more about the entrapment defense, a mountain of literature exists on the subject and continues to grow. Although most of the books and articles do not directly address North Carolina law, some may provide useful analysis and authority. A list of references appears at the end of this book. By far the most complete work is Paul Marcus's excellent one-volume treatise on entrapment, on which I have relied heavily in interpreting the various components of the defense.

I want to thank those who helped me produce this book. Robert Farb and Jessica Smith, my colleagues at the Institute of Government, and Tom Maher and Daniel Pollitt, very fine criminal defense lawyers, read and offered helpful comments on earlier drafts. Melissa Twomey, Carol Offen, and Nancy Dooly edited the book, Robby Poore designed it, and others at the Institute contributed to the book's production and distribution. As in everything, my family was always there to support me.

I welcome comments about the book. They can be sent to me at the Institute of Government, CB #3330, Knapp Building, The University of North Carolina at Chapel Hill, Chapel Hill, North Carolina 27599-3330. I can also be reached by e-mail at rubin@iogmail.iog.unc.edu.

John Rubin

Chapel Hill
Spring 2001

1 History of the Entrapment Defense

1 History of the Entrapment Defense

The entrapment defense is relatively new in North Carolina. Until the 1930s, the North Carolina courts apparently did not recognize that the methods used by law enforcement officers to induce a person to violate the law could serve as a potential defense in an ensuing prosecution. For example, if a person illegally sold whiskey to an officer, a recurring fact pattern in the early 1900s, the person could be convicted regardless of the temptations placed by the officer in the person's path.[1]

The North Carolina courts began to soften their position after the United States Supreme Court's first entrapment decision in 1932, *Sorrells v. United States*.[2] Following the lead of several lower federal court decisions, the Court in *Sorrells* recognized entrapment as a defense concerning conduct that otherwise would have amounted to a violation of federal law. In this Prohibition-era case, a government agent had coaxed the defendant into obtaining and providing to the agent a half-gallon of alcohol. Finding that "the act for which defendant was prosecuted was instigated by the prohibition agent . . . [and] that defendant had no previous disposition to commit it," the Court threw out the conviction.[3] The Court reasoned that Congress did not intend for its statutes to be enforced by inducing otherwise innocent people into violations.

The *Sorrells* decision was not based on the United States Constitution. It rested instead on the Court's interpretation of federal law and, accordingly, did not require state courts to follow suit and recognize entrapment as a defense. Nevertheless, the high court's views carried great weight. Soon after *Sorrells*, the North Carolina Supreme Court

---

1. *See* State v. Hopkins, 154 N.C. 622, 624, 70 S.E. 394, 394–95 (1911) (methods employed by police did not affect whether defendant had violated law prohibiting sale of whiskey); State v. Smith, 152 N.C. 798, 67 S.E. 508 (1910) (to same effect); *see also* State v. Ice & Fuel Co., 166 N.C. 366, 370, 81 S.E. 737, 739 (1914) (quoting *Hopkins* and *Smith* with approval).

2. 287 U.S. 435 (1932).

3. *Id.* at 441.

began hinting at the possibility of recognizing an entrapment defense under state law.[4] In 1948, in *State v. Love,* the court recognized the defense explicitly.[5] *Love* and other North Carolina decisions echo the policies articulated by the United States Supreme Court for prohibiting the conviction of someone who has been entrapped—upholding the integrity of the administration of justice, setting limits on permissible police conduct, and protecting otherwise innocent people.[6]

In the years following *Love,* the North Carolina appellate courts issued several decisions on entrapment. During the past decade, however, the defense seemed to fall into disuse, although the pace of decisions has picked up somewhat in recent years. Since 1990, only a few reported decisions in North Carolina, all at the court of appeals level, have dealt with entrapment.[7] The North Carolina Supreme Court has not addressed the subject since 1982.[8]

The reason for this apparent decline is not entirely clear, although it may be traceable to the low esteem in which the criminal defense bar holds the entrapment defense. One commentator has advised that the entrapment defense be used only in "desperate circumstances where no other defense is possible."[9] Another has remarked that the defense "can be raised only at a great price to the defendant."[10]

What explains such a negative assessment? One possibility is that entrapment, more so than other defenses, is an all-or-nothing proposition. A defendant who expects to maintain any credibility with a jury

---

4. *See* State v. Hughes, 208 N.C. 542, 554–55, 181 S.E. 737, 744–45 (1935) (discussing federal entrapment cases with approval, but finding no violation "in law or morals" in manner in which defendant was caught); State v. Godwin, 227 N.C. 449, 452, 42 S.E.2d 617, 619 (1947) (questioning state's case against defendant because of officer's "persistent entreaty and duplicity"); *see also* Albert Coates, *Limitations on Investigating Officers,* 15 N.C. L. REV. 229, 229–31 (1936–37) (reviewing North Carolina cases on entrapment).

5. 229 N.C. 99, 100–02, 47 S.E.2d 712, 713–14 (1948); *see also* State v. Stanley, 288 N.C. 19, 27, 215 S.E.2d 589, 595 (1975) (noting that *Love* was first case to recognize entrapment as defense in North Carolina).

6. *See Love,* 229 N.C. at 101, 47 S.E.2d at 714 (discussing notions of purity and fairness); State v. Hageman, 307 N.C. 1, 29, 296 S.E.2d 433, 449 (1982) (emphasizing limits on permissible police conduct and need for safeguards for innocent citizens); State v. Whisnant, 36 N.C. App. 252, 254, 243 S.E.2d 395, 396 (1978) ("main purpose of the entrapment defense is to regulate government activity in investigating crimes").

7. There have been five reported decisions on entrapment since 1990—one in 2001, two in 1999, and the others in 1997 and 1990. *See* State v. Thompson, 142 N.C. App. __, 543 S.E.2d 160 (2001); State v. Broome, 136 N.C. App. 82, 523 S.E.2d 448 (1999); State v. McCaslin, 132 N.C. App. 352, 511 S.E.2d 347 (1999); State v. Davis, 126 N.C. App. 415, 485 S.E.2d 329 (1997); State v. Clemmons, 100 N.C. App. 286, 396 S.E.2d 616 (1990).

8. *See Hageman,* 307 N.C. at 29, 296 S.E.2d at 449.

9. Ben A. Hardy, *The Traps of Entrapment,* 3 AM. J. CRIM. L. 165, 165 (1974).

10. MODEL PENAL CODE AND COMMENTARIES § 2.13 cmt. 6 (1985).

can hardly claim, "I didn't do it, but if I did, I was entrapped."[11] The defendant must trust that the jury will find, based primarily on the actions of law enforcement personnel, reason to excuse conduct that would otherwise amount to a crime.

A defendant claiming entrapment also must carry the baggage of his or her past, again to a greater degree than those asserting other defenses. In many jurisdictions, including North Carolina, the entrapment defense fails if the jury finds that the defendant was "predisposed" to commit the offense. To show this predisposition, the prosecution may be permitted to engage in a fairly searching inquiry into the defendant's past misdeeds. Although evidence of prior bad acts does not preclude the use of an entrapment defense, it may turn a jury against the defendant, even in the face of unsavory police conduct. The federal version of entrapment is comparable to North Carolina's version of the defense and presents many of the same pitfalls, yet seems to have greater vitality. The United States Supreme Court has issued six major entrapment decisions in federal prosecutions.[12] Each year several decisions on entrapment are issued by the federal circuit courts of appeal.[13]

The greater number of federal appellate decisions on entrapment does not necessarily warrant the conclusion that the defense is underutilized in state court. Various reasons—the types of cases prosecuted or the nature and extent of undercover operations, for example—may serve to make entrapment a more appropriate defense to federal prosecutions, whereas other defense strategies may stand a greater chance of success in state prosecutions. Nevertheless, the steady growth

---

11. Whether as a legal matter a defendant may deny the charges and also claim entrapment is discussed *infra* § 4.3.

12. The decisions, in chronological order, are: Sorrells v. United States, 287 U.S. 435 (1932) (first recognizing entrapment as defense); Sherman v. United States, 356 U.S. 369 (1958) (reaffirming availability of entrapment defense and finding that defendant had been entrapped as matter of law, notwithstanding that he had been previously convicted of other crimes); United States v. Russell, 411 U.S. 423 (1973) (suggesting that outrageous government conduct may violate Due Process and warrant dismissal of charges even if defendant is predisposed to commit offense and thus unable to assert entrapment defense successfully); Hampton v. United States, 425 U.S. 484 (1976) (finding that defendant was not entrapped as matter of law but continuing to recognize possibility that outrageous government conduct may violate Due Process and warrant dismissal); Mathews v. United States, 485 U.S. 58 (1988) (holding under federal law that defendant may raise entrapment defense even though he or she denies having committed crime); Jacobson v. United States, 503 U.S. 540 (1992) (finding entrapment as matter of law and emphasizing that defendant's predisposition is measured as of time of initial government contact, not time of government's solicitation of illegal acts). The U.S. Supreme Court has addressed entrapment contentions in other cases, but the decisions are not as significant as those above. *See, e.g.,* Osborn v. United States, 385 U.S. 323 (1966) (defendant not entrapped as matter of law); Lopez v. United States, 373 U.S. 427 (1963) (to same effect); Masciale v. United States, 356 U.S. 386 (1958) (to same effect).

13. For recent Fourth Circuit decisions on entrapment, *see generally* CARL HORN, FOURTH CIRCUIT CRIMINAL HANDBOOK: 2001 EDITION § 244, at 281-82 (2000).

in federal decisions suggests that it is worth reconsidering the potential utility of raising an entrapment defense in North Carolina.[14]

The aim of the following chapters is to anticipate the main issues that may arise in cases involving entrapment claims in North Carolina. The focus, of course, is North Carolina law, but federal decisions and the decisions of other states are examined for additional guidance. Federal decisions in particular are an important resource in interpreting unsettled areas of North Carolina law. North Carolina's version of entrapment, although not mandated by federal law, is rooted in it; and, in the larger and more comprehensive body of federal entrapment decisions, the courts have explored many problems yet to be addressed in North Carolina.

---

14. Failure to raise entrapment in the appropriate circumstances may constitute ineffective assistance of counsel. *See generally* Gregory G. Sarno, Annotation, *Adequacy of Defense Counsel's Representation of Criminal Client Regarding Entrapment Defense,* 8 A.L.R.4th 1160 (1981); Capps v. Sullivan, 921 F.2d 260 (10th Cir. 1990) (finding that trial attorney's failure to request entrapment instruction, which was supported by law and evidence, constituted ineffective assistance of counsel).

2   Rules of Entrapment

§ 2.1   Effect of Defense   9

§ 2.2   The Subjective and Objective Tests   11

§ 2.3   What Constitutes Inducement?   13
- (a)   Generally   13
- (b)   Inducement Not Found   14
- (c)   Inducement Found   16

§ 2.4   Who Are Government Agents?   18
- (a)   Generally   18
- (b)   Private Persons   19
- (c)   Unwitting Intermediaries   21

§ 2.5   What Constitutes Predisposition?   23
- (a)   Generally   23
- (b)   Relevant Factors   24
- (c)   Timing of Government Contact   28

2 Rules of Entrapment

§ 2.1 EFFECT OF DEFENSE

When an entrapment defense is successful, the defendant must be acquitted of the offense charged.[1] While entrapment is raised most often as a defense in drug prosecutions, over the years the courts have recognized it as a basis for acquittal of many types of charges, including

- drug offenses;[2]
- theft offenses;[3]
- bribery;[4]
- perjury;[5]
- alcohol violations;[6]

---

1. *See* State v. Caldwell, 249 N.C. 56, 59, 105 S.E.2d 189, 191 (1958) (verdict of not guilty must be returned if state entrapped defendant); State v. Wallace, 246 N.C. 445, 446–47, 98 S.E.2d 473, 474 (1957) (court should have charged jury that if it found that defendant had been entrapped, it must return verdict of not guilty). Ordinarily entrapment is a complete defense to criminal liability, but in some instances it may support a reduction in the level of offense. Defendants may claim that they were induced to commit a greater offense than they were predisposed to commit—for example, although willing to engage in small drug transactions, they became involved in much larger quantities at the government's urging. If successful, such a claim may be a defense to the greater offense but would leave the defendant open to conviction of the lesser. *See infra* § 3.4 notes 56–57 and accompanying text.

2. *See* State v. Stanley, 288 N.C. 19, 215 S.E.2d 589 (1975); *see also* Daniel E. Feld, Annotation, *Modern Status of the Law Concerning Entrapment to Commit Narcotics Offense—Federal Cases*, 22 A.L.R. FED. 731 (1975); Daniel E. Feld, Annotation, *Modern Status of the Law Concerning Entrapment to Commit Narcotics Offense—State Cases*, 62 A.L.R.3d 110 (1975); Annotation, *Entrapment as Defense to Charge of Selling or Supplying Narcotics where Government Agents Supplied Narcotics to Defendant and Purchased Them from Him*, 9 A.L.R.5th 464 (1975) (known as "full-circle transactions").

3. *See* State v. Hageman, 307 N.C. 1, 296 S.E.2d 433 (1982) (receiving stolen goods); State v. Luster, 306 N.C. 566, 295 S.E.2d 421 (1982) (larceny); D. E. Ytreberg, Annotation, *Larceny: Entrapment or Consent*, 10 A.L.R.3d 1121 (1966).

4. *See* State v. Bryant, 251 N.C. 217, 110 S.E.2d 892 (1959); D. E. Buckner, Annotation, *Entrapment to Commit Bribery or Offer to Bribe*, 69 A.L.R.2d 1397 (1960).

5. *See* United States v. Sarihifard, 155 F.3d 301, 308–09 (4th Cir. 1998).

6. *See* State v. Wallace, 246 N.C. 445, 98 S.E.2d 473 (1957); State v. Love, 229 N.C. 99, 47 S.E.2d 712 (1948); E. LeFevre, Annotation, *Entrapment to Commit Offense against Laws Regulating Sales of Liquor*, 55 A.L.R.2d 1322 (1957).

- fish and game violations;[7]
- driving while impaired and other traffic offenses;[8]
- obscenity and prostitution crimes;[9]
- gambling offenses;[10] and
- weapons offenses.[11]

It has been suggested that, as a matter of policy, entrapment should not be available as a defense to violent offenses.[12] In the few North Carolina cases involving conduct that posed a threat of physical injury (but where such injury was not actually inflicted), the court in each case found the evidence of entrapment insufficient to support the relief requested but did not reject entrapment as a possible defense.[13]

Like most other defenses, North Carolina's entrapment defense is ordinarily raised at trial and, if the defendant presents sufficient evidence in support of the defense, it must be submitted to the jury for decision.[14] In some instances, the evidence of entrapment may be so

---

7. *See* R. W. Gascoyne, Annotation, *Entrapment with respect to Violation of Fish and Game Laws,* 75 A.L.R.2d 709 (1961).

8. *See* State v. McCaslin, 132 N.C. App. 352, 511 S.E.2d 347 (1999); State v. Bailey, 93 N.C. App. 721, 379 S.E.2d 266 (1989); State v. Green, 27 N.C. App. 491, 219 S.E.2d 529 (1975); Sara L. Johnson, Annotation, *Entrapment to Commit Traffic Offense,* 34 A.L.R.4th 1167 (1984).

9. *See* State v. Demott, 26 N.C. App. 14, 214 S.E.2d 781 (1975) (prostitution offenses); Gregory G. Sarno, Annotation, *Entrapment Defense in Sex Offense Prosecutions,* 12 A.L.R.4th 413 (1982) (prostitution offenses, consensual homosexual acts and sodomy, and miscellaneous acts of sexual nature); J. A. Bock, Annotation, *Entrapment to Commit Offense against Obscenity Laws,* 77 A.L.R.2d 792 (1961).

10. *See* R. P. Davis, Annotation, *Entrapment to Commit Offense with respect to Gambling or Lotteries,* 31 A.L.R.2d 1212 (1953).

11. *See* United States v. Cannon, 886 F. Supp. 705 (D.N.D. 1995) (purchase of machine gun), *rev'd on other grounds,* 88 F.3d 1495 (8th Cir. 1996).

12. *See* MODEL PENAL CODE & COMMENTARIES § 2.13 & cmt. 8 (1985) (entrapment should not be available as defense to offenses that inflict or threaten bodily injury); *see also* Sorrells v. United States, 287 U.S. 435, 451 (1932) (court declines to decide whether crime may be "so heinous or revolting" as to preclude entrapment defense).

13. *See* State v. Fletcher, 279 N.C. 85, 92–94, 181 S.E.2d 405, 411–12 (1971) (in armed robbery prosecution, entrapment evidence was insufficient to require disclosure of identity of confidential informant); State v. Caldwell, 249 N.C. 56, 105 S.E.2d 189 (1958) (in prosecution for conspiracy and attempt to bomb school, entrapment evidence was insufficient to require nonsuit); State v. Burnette, 242 N.C. 164, 87 S.E.2d 191 (1955) (in prosecution for assault with intent to commit rape, entrapment evidence was insufficient to require nonsuit). Even if entrapment is not a defense to a particular crime, related defenses may still be available. *See infra* § 3.1(b) (discussing consent as defense to physical and sexual assaults); § 3.2(c) (discussing "innocent intent" defense in armed robbery case); § 3.3(a) note 39 (discussing possible grounds for Due Process defense).

14. North Carolina uses the subjective test of entrapment, which is considered a matter for the jury when the evidence is in dispute. For a discussion of the evidentiary showing required for submission of instructions to the jury on entrapment, *see infra* § 6.2(b). Jurisdictions using an objective test of entrapment, discussed *infra* § 2.2, generally view that test as one involving a question of law for the judge to resolve. *See* PAUL MARCUS, THE ENTRAPMENT DEFENSE § 5.06, at 184–85 (2d ed. 1995).

strong as to warrant dismissal of the charges at the close of trial.[15] Rarely, if ever, however, would it be appropriate for a judge to sustain or reject the defense pretrial.[16] Some North Carolina cases imply, but do not actually hold, that a defendant may move before trial to suppress evidence discovered as the result of entrapment of the defendant. The legal basis for such a motion is unclear.[17]

Entrapment principles may also play a part in sentencing proceedings after trial. For example, a failed entrapment defense may have mitigating value at sentencing.[18]

§ 2.2 THE SUBJECTIVE AND OBJECTIVE TESTS

To prevail on a claim of entrapment in North Carolina, a defendant must meet a two-pronged test. The defendant must show that

1. law enforcement officers or their agents, by trickery, fraud, or persuasion, induced the defendant to commit the charged offense; *and*
2. the defendant was not predisposed to commit the offense.[19]

This formulation places North Carolina in the "subjective" camp of entrapment because the second element of the test focuses on the

---

15. *See infra* § 6.2(c) (showing required for nonsuit).

16. *See* United States v. Fadel, 844 F.2d 1425, 1430–31 (10th Cir. 1988) (although leaving open possibility, court states that pretrial resolution of entrapment defense is seldom appropriate because it is so intertwined with issue of intent); *see also infra* § 2.5(a) (discussing factual nature of predisposition inquiry). In contrast, most courts have held that the Due Process defense of outrageous conduct is resolved by the judge, not by the jury, and may be heard before trial. *See infra* § 3.3(b).

17. *See* State v. Murrell, 54 N.C. App. 342, 283 S.E.2d 173 (1981) (suggesting possibility of suppression motion); *see also* State v. Wooten, 55 N.C. App. 530, 533, 286 S.E.2d 635, 638 (1982) (defendant argued that his statements to officer were result of entrapment and therefore inadmissible); State v. Hendrix, 19 N.C. App. 99, 101, 197 S.E.2d 892, 893 (1973) (defendant argued that evidence was illegally obtained by means of entrapment and therefore was inadmissible). *But cf.* United States v. Al-Talib, 55 F.3d 923, 929 (4th Cir. 1995) (finding that there is no such thing as "venue entrapment"—that is, drawing of person to particular venue to commit offense—and refusing to dismiss case for trial in another venue).

18. For a discussion of the potential mitigating value of entrapment principles at sentencing, including a variant of the entrapment defense known as "sentencing entrapment," *see infra* § 3.4.

19. *See, e.g.,* State v. Burnette, 242 N.C. 164, 169, 87 S.E.2d 191, 194 (1955) ("where the criminal intent and design originates in the mind of one other than the defendant, and the defendant is, by persuasion, trickery or fraud, incited and induced to commit the crime charged in order to prosecute him for it, when he would not have committed the crime, except for such incitements and inducements, these circumstances constitute entrapment and a valid defense"); State v. Hageman, 307 N.C. 1, 28–29, 296 S.E.2d 433, 449 (1982) (to same effect).

mental state of the defendant.[20] One of the principal rationales for the subjective approach is that a person who is not predisposed to commit an offense, but who does so at the instigation of the government, does not have the guilty mind necessary for conviction. On the other hand, in most cases a defendant who is predisposed to commit the offense will not be successful in asserting entrapment regardless of the government's conduct.[21]

In this basic respect, North Carolina's approach to entrapment tracks federal law. In *Sorrells v. United States*[22] and *Sherman v. United States,*[23] the United States Supreme Court adopted the subjective test of entrapment for federal cases (sometimes called the *Sorrells-Sherman* test). A majority of state courts also use a subjective test of entrapment.[24]

A substantial minority of jurisdictions, and a majority of commentators, favor an "objective" test of entrapment.[25] The dissenters in *Sorrells* and *Sherman* also advocated an objective test of entrapment. Although formulations of the objective test vary, they share a critical feature: All focus on the potential effect of the government's tactics on an "average" or "normally law-abiding" or "reasonable" person. The objective test does not depend on the predisposition of the particular defendant. For example, under the Model Penal Code, entrapment occurs if the government induces a person to commit an offense by employing methods that create a substantial risk that the offense would be committed by a law-abiding person.[26] Public policy considerations underlie the objective approach: By barring conviction, the objective test prevents the government from benefiting from its excesses.

Is one test more favorable to defendants than the other? Theoretically, no. To prevail under the objective test, the defendant must show significant overreaching by the government. Under the subjective test, although

---

20. *See* State v. Luster, 306 N.C. 566, 575, 295 S.E.2d 421, 426 (1982) (defendant's predisposition to commit the crime is the central inquiry); Hampton v. United States, 425 U.S. 484, 488 (1976) (subjective version of entrapment defense "focuses on the intent or predisposition of the defendant to commit the crime rather than on the conduct of the Government's agents"); United States v. Hunt, 749 F.2d 1078, 1085 (4th Cir. 1984) ("the essential element of the entrapment defense is the defendant's lack of predisposition to commit the crime charged").

21. If the government's conduct is considered sufficiently outrageous—a difficult standard to meet—the defendant may have a defense to the charges regardless of his or her predisposition. *See infra* § 3.3(a) (discussing Due Process defense, which rests on principles related to but distinct from those underlying entrapment defense).

22. 287 U.S. 435 (1932).

23. 356 U.S. 369 (1958).

24. *See* 2 WAYNE R. LaFAVE ET AL., CRIMINAL PROCEDURE § 5.2(a), at 406–07 (2d ed. 1999).

25. *See id.* § 5.2(b), at 410.

26. MODEL PENAL CODE AND COMMENTARIES § 2.13 & cmt. 3 (1985).

government inducement is a required element of the defense, the standard is not as demanding. The focus instead is on whether the defendant was predisposed to commit the offense. Consequently, government actions that would not be sufficiently egregious to support an entrapment defense under the objective test could constitute entrapment under the subjective test if the defendant was not predisposed to commit the offense.[27]

In practice, however, the prosecution may enjoy a significant advantage under the subjective test. To show the defendant's predisposition, courts have given the prosecution considerable leeway in exploring the defendant's past misdeeds. Such evidence may so color the jurors' impression of the defendant as to overwhelm any concerns about the government's conduct.[28]

§ 2.3   WHAT CONSTITUTES INDUCEMENT?

To satisfy the first prong of the subjective test of entrapment—government inducement—the defendant must show that

- he or she was induced to commit the crime, and
- the person who induced the defendant to do so was acting on behalf of the government.

Conduct constituting inducement is discussed in this section; the next section discusses the type of person who meets the definition of government agent.

(a)   Generally

General pronouncements about the meaning of inducement appear throughout North Carolina appellate decisions, the most common one being that the government must engage in some act of fraud, trickery, encouragement, persuasion, or importunity.[29] Such statements reveal little, however, about the sort of government conduct that rises to the level of inducement. Perhaps the best way to begin exploring this topic is by observing that the government's actions must surpass one threshold but not necessarily another, higher one.

Thus, on the one hand, the government's conduct must surpass the threshold of "mere opportunity." The courts have often stated that the government does not induce a defendant to act merely by affording him

---

27. For a further discussion of the meaning of inducement under North Carolina law, *see infra* § 2.3.

28. For a further discussion of the admissibility of the defendant's prior conduct on the question of predisposition, *see infra* § 5.1.

29. *See, e.g.,* State v. Burnette, 242 N.C. 164, 169, 87 S.E.2d 191, 194 (1955); State v. Love, 229 N.C. 99, 101–02, 47 S.E.2d 712, 714 (1948); State v. Davis, 38 N.C. App. 672, 676, 248 S.E.2d 883, 886 (1978).

or her the opportunity to commit a crime, by allowing a crime to go forward, or by setting a trap.[30] As one court put it, the government's conduct must consist of an " 'opportunity' plus something else," such as repeated or excessive solicitations.[31] On the other hand, to show inducement under the subjective test of entrapment, the defendant need not show that the government's conduct amounted to the sort of unreasonable or objectionable conduct required under the objective test of entrapment, which focuses on whether the government's conduct exceeded acceptable bounds.[32]

To understand what amounts to "opportunity plus," one must look at specific decisions addressing the sufficiency of the evidence presented by the defendant. Sufficiency issues may arise in various contexts. The court may have to determine whether the defendant has produced sufficient evidence to require the government to disclose the identity of a confidential informant or to warrant instructions to the jury on entrapment or dismissal of the charges altogether. Different standards apply to these inquiries, discussed in later chapters, but together the cases shed some light on the meaning of inducement.

(b) Inducement Not Found

The North Carolina appellate courts have found in a number of cases that the government did not induce the defendant to commit the charged offense, but instead merely afforded him or her the "opportunity" to do so. The following discussion identifies recurring fact patterns that the courts have found to fall short of inducement.[33]

Mere Solicitation. In *State v. Martin,* an undercover officer contacted the defendant about buying cocaine and gave the defendant money for the cocaine. The officer made no effort to ingratiate himself with the defendant, made no promises, and offered no gifts. Using his own sources, the defendant obtained the cocaine for the officer. The

---

30. *See* State v. Walker, 295 N.C. 510, 515, 246 S.E.2d 748, 751 (1978); State v. Caldwell, 249 N.C. 56, 59, 105 S.E.2d 189, 191 (1958).

31. United States v. Gendron, 18 F.3d 955, 961 (1st Cir. 1994) (Breyer, J.).

32. For a comparison of the subjective and objective tests, *see supra* § 2.2. In analyzing the inducement element of the subjective test of entrapment, some courts appear to have injected an objective component. The Fourth Circuit, for example, has stated that the government's entreaties must be enough to induce a "reasonably firm" person to succumb. *See* United States v. DeVore, 423 F.2d 1069, 1072 (4th Cir. 1970). Such an approach seems more demanding than contemplated by the subjective test, although the required showing still appears to be well less than that required under the objective test of entrapment. *See generally* MARCUS, *supra* note 14, § 4.04, at 116 (although courts do not completely agree on level of evidence needed to show inducement under subjective test of entrapment, "it is fair to say that the burden is a limited one").

33. Not all decisions fit within a particular category. *See, e.g.,* State v. Walker, 295 N.C. 510, 246 S.E.2d 748 (1978) (majority upholds denial of entrapment instructions, finding that officers' request that defendant obtain information on drug trade did not constitute inducement that defendant engage in sale of drugs to undercover agent; dis-

court found that the government had engaged in mere solicitation of the defendant and did not induce him to commit a crime.[34]

Setting a Trap. In *State v. Coleman,* officers placed an ad in a newspaper offering to sell a woman's article of clothing. The defendant called the telephone number and, when a woman answered, he used indecent language toward her. The court found that the officers had merely set a trap for the defendant, which did not constitute inducement.[35]

Allowing Completion of Crime. In *State v. Rosario,* a courier attempted to deliver a package of cocaine to the defendant. Officers intercepted the delivery, searched the package, and found the cocaine. The officers then prepared a duplicate box with approximately the same amount of cocaine and directed the courier to deliver the box as originally planned to the defendant, who accepted delivery. The court found that the officers merely allowed an ongoing crime to be completed.[36]

In *State v. Fletcher,* officers received information that the defendants were going to rob the victim at the victim's business. Officers concealed themselves at the business and arrested the defendants as they tried to rob the victim. The court found that the officers only acted upon information they had received about a possible crime and did not induce the defendants' commission of the crime.[37]

---

sent argues that, although government did not expressly tell defendant to sell drugs, government led defendant to believe that he needed to comply with agent's request for drugs as part of defendant's earlier agreement with law enforcement).

34. 77 N.C. App. 61, 67, 334 S.E.2d 459, 462–63 (1985) (instructions properly denied); *see also* State v. Kilgore, 246 N.C. 455, 455–56, 98 S.E.2d 346, 347 (1957) (any error in entrapment instructions given by trial court was not prejudicial because there was no evidence of entrapment; undercover officer merely went to defendant's home seeking to buy beer, and defendant illegally sold beer to officer); State v. Duncan, 75 N.C. App. 38, 46–47, 330 S.E.2d 481, 487–88 (1985) (nonsuit properly denied; jury could reasonably infer that officer's solicitations to buy cocaine provided no more than opportunity for defendant to commit offenses); State v. Stanback, 19 N.C. App. 375, 376, 198 S.E.2d 759, 760 (1973) (instructions properly denied; undercover agent merely went to defendant's apartment and asked to buy marijuana).

35. 270 N.C. 357, 362–63, 154 S.E.2d 485, 489 (1967) (exclusion of evidence offered by defendant, which was purportedly relevant to entrapment defense, was not error); *see also* State v. Burnette, 242 N.C. 164, 87 S.E.2d 191 (1955) (defendant telephoned woman and said he wanted her, and at officer's direction woman agreed to meet with defendant, who then assaulted her; nonsuit properly denied).

36. 93 N.C. App. 627, 635–37, 379 S.E.2d 434, 438–39 (1989) (request for instructions on entrapment and motion for nonsuit properly denied). The court in *Rosario* noted that had the officers increased the amount of cocaine in the package and thus exposed the defendant to higher penalties, the defendant may have had a defense to the enhanced offense. For a further discussion of what is sometimes called "sentencing entrapment," *see infra* § 3.4.

37. 279 N.C. 85, 92–94, 181 S.E.2d 405, 411–12 (1971) (no error in refusing to require government to disclose identity of its informant); *see also* State v. Bailey, 93 N.C. App. 721, 379 S.E.2d 266 (1989) (intoxicated defendant approached officer seeking assistance in locating his truck, officer pointed out location of truck, and defendant got into his truck and drove away; officer did not induce defendant to drive while impaired, and defendant was not entitled to instruction on entrapment, even assuming officer did not attempt to stop defendant from driving).

(c)   Inducement Found

The cases discussed below held that the government actions constituted inducement within the meaning of the first prong of entrapment or, at least, that the evidence of inducement was sufficient to warrant jury instructions on entrapment or some other ruling favorable to the defendant. Although these cases cannot be neatly categorized, certain factors can be identified that help distinguish government actions that merely afford a person the opportunity to commit a crime and those that conceivably could induce a person to engage in criminal activity.

Significant Factors. In finding inducement, the courts have relied on evidence showing that officers or other government agents

- exploited a special relationship with the defendant, such as using a friendship or other relationship as a means for the government agent to ingratiate himself or herself with the defendant;
- took advantage of the defendant's youth, financial circumstances, or other vulnerabilities;
- employed various forms of persuasion, such as making repeated requests, promises, or threats;
- assisted the defendant in committing the crime, such as locating suppliers or providing transportation; or
- made misrepresentations to the defendant (other than as to the identity of the officer or other government agent).[38]

These factors can be seen in the cases discussed below under "Illustrative Cases."

Another factor that may bolster a showing of inducement is the use of informants by the government. Like undercover officers, informants may do no more than provide a defendant with an opportunity to commit an offense, which does not in itself constitute inducement. The courts have found, however, that informants have a tendency to overreach. The Fourth Circuit has observed in drug cases:

> The payment of contingent fees to informants, the use of informants who are drug addicts, promises of immunity and pay-offs in drugs create a self-interest on the part of the informant. This self-interest in "making a buy" may lead to excessive appeals to the seller's sympathies or other unconscionable tactics.[39]

---

38. The courts have held that deception by undercover agents about their identity may be the only practicable way for them to interact with a suspect and does not by itself bar prosecution on entrapment grounds. *See, e.g.,* State v. Salame, 24 N.C. App. 1, 6–9, 210 S.E.2d 77, 81–83 (1974) (playacting by undercover officers during drug deal did not compel nonsuit on entrapment grounds; question of entrapment was for jury).

39. McLawhorn v. North Carolina, 484 F.2d 1, 7 n.18 (4th Cir. 1973) (granting habeas petition for trial court's failure to require disclosure of identity of informant), *vacating* 16 N.C.

Illustrative Cases. The following cases illustrate the range of actions that the courts may find to constitute inducement. They also show that evidence of varying strength may be sufficient to show inducement.

State v. Stanley illustrates a particularly strong showing of inducement. There, the uncontradicted evidence showed that a twenty-eight-year-old police officer, posing as an army sergeant, ingratiated himself with the seventeen-year-old defendant and gained his confidence. The officer sought out the defendant's companionship, continually called him at home, allowed him to drive the officer's car, and assured his parents that he would look after their son. Once he had established a "big brother" relationship with the defendant, the officer asked him to get some LSD. The court held that this evidence supported a finding of entrapment as a matter of law, requiring dismissal of the charges.[40]

In *State v. Jamerson,* the defendant's evidence showed that an undercover agent and an informant went to see the defendant, a college student known by the informant, and asked him to sell them some drugs. When the defendant said he didn't have any, the agent and informant asked him to find some and said they would be back in three hours. The defendant made no effort to comply with the request and, when the agent and informant returned, the defendant again said that he had no drugs. The agent said that he was an addict and was desperate, and the informant said he knew of another student who would sell drugs to the defendant. The informant offered the defendant $15 to make the purchase, and the informant and agent drove the defendant to the campus, where the defendant made the purchase from the person identified by the informant. The court found that this evidence warranted an instruction to the jury on entrapment.[41]

App. 153, 191 S.E.2d 410 (1972); *see also* Sherman v. United States, 356 U.S. 369 (1958) (informant had several conversations with defendant about their mutual attempts to overcome addiction, then made repeated requests to defendant to supply him with narcotics because of his suffering; court condemned activities of informant and found entrapment as matter of law), *cited with approval in* State v. Stanley, 288 N.C. 19, 29–31, 215 S.E.2d 589, 596–97 (1975).

40. 288 N.C. 19, 215 S.E.2d 589 (1975); *see also* State v. Board, 296 N.C. 652, 252 S.E.2d 803 (1979) (on facts strikingly similar to *Stanley,* majority of court ordered dismissal of charges on grounds unrelated to entrapment; relying on *Stanley,* three-judge concurrence stated it would dismiss charges on entrapment grounds).

41. 64 N.C. App. 301, 303–04, 307 S.E.2d 436, 437–38 (1983). Unlike *Stanley,* dismissal of the charges would not have been appropriate in *Jamerson* because, contrary to the defendant's evidence, the state showed that the defendant willingly sold drugs to the informant and undercover officer. When the material evidence conflicts, the question of entrapment is for the jury to resolve. *See infra* § 6.2(c) (discussing standard for nonsuit).

Jamerson cites as examples of government inducement a number of cases in which the trial court found the evidence sufficient to warrant instructions on entrapment. *See, e.g.,* State v. Grier, 51 N.C. App. 209, 275 S.E.2d 560 (1981) (after ingratiating himself by frequently visiting defendant and giving her presents, undercover agent supplied money for drug purchase and drove defendant to home of supplier); State v. Hartman, 49 N.C. App. 83, 270 S.E.2d 609 (1980) (defendant was promised job if he sold LSD that afternoon); State v. Braun, 31 N.C. App. 101, 228 S.E.2d 466 (1976) (agent picked up defendant who was hitchhiking, asked defendant for marijuana, telephoned him next day, and drove defendant to third person's home where defendant obtained marijuana for agent).

In *State v. Sanders,* an informant approached the defendant about participating in a scheme to sell to the informant's rich acquaintance a substance that they would say was cocaine but actually would be baking soda. The informant specified the dates on which the sales would take place, procured the substance, which in fact was cocaine, and brought it to the defendant, who sold it to the acquaintance, an undercover officer. The defendant was charged with various offenses involving sale of cocaine. The court found that the criminal design originated with the informant, not with the defendant, and that the trial court erred in refusing to instruct on entrapment.[42]

In *State v. Whisnant,* a co-worker called the defendant and said that a friend of her husband's needed to buy some drugs for pain. The defendant said that she only had some medication of her own. The co-worker and an undercover officer thereafter went to the defendant's apartment, where she agreed to sell the medication for $.50 per capsule and $1.00 per tablet. The medication contained codeine, a controlled substance, and the defendant was charged with sale and delivery. The trial court instructed on the entrapment defense, but added that the defense was not available if the defendant was induced to act by someone other than a law enforcement officer. The court of appeals ordered a new trial, finding that the trial court should have instructed that entrapment was available if an officer or agent induced the criminal acts charged. The court of appeals stated that the evidence supported such an instruction because it showed that the co-worker had been acting as an agent of the undercover officer and in that capacity had engaged in some inducement of the defendant to make the illegal sale.[43]

A number of other decisions have found that the government's conduct amounted to inducement within the meaning of entrapment law.[44]

§ 2.4 WHO ARE GOVERNMENT AGENTS?

(a) Generally

There is "no defense of private entrapment." Solicitations by a person who is not acting on behalf of the government, no matter how

---

42. 95 N.C. App. 56, 381 S.E.2d 827 (1989) (because defendant did not object, trial court's failure to give entrapment instruction was reviewed under plain error standard; new trial not required). Undercover operations in which government agents both supply and purchase drugs from a defendant have been called "full-circle transactions." *See* annotations cited *supra* note 2.

43. 36 N.C. App. 252, 243 S.E.2d 395 (1978). For a further discussion of whether private persons may be considered agents of the government, *see infra* § 2.4.

44. *See* State v. Blackwell, 67 N.C. App. 432, 313 S.E.2d 797 (1984) (defendant sought out information about and bought drugs for undercover officer because defendant needed job and officer implied that he could get defendant one; trial court erred in failing to instruct on entrapment); State v. Walker, 66 N.C. App. 367, 311 S.E.2d 329 (1984) (informant and defendant were lifelong friends, informant introduced defendant

tempting, will not support an entrapment defense.[45] For example, if two people commit a burglary, one burglar cannot escape prosecution on entrapment grounds by claiming that the other burglar induced him or her to commit the crime. The inducement must come from someone acting for or on behalf of the government—in other words, a government agent within the meaning of entrapment law.

Law-enforcement officers, including undercover officers, are certainly considered agents of the government.[46] In some circumstances, a private person may be considered an agent of the government. When the inducement comes from a private person, however, two questions may arise. The first and most common is whether the person was acting on the government's behalf or on his or her own. If the person was acting at the behest of a government official, a second question may arise—namely, whether the person may be considered an agent of the government if he or she was unaware of the official's identity. Each question is addressed below.

(b) Private Persons

Factors in Determining Agency. In determining whether a private person is acting on the government's behalf, the courts consider all the circumstances of the relationship between the parties. Precise rules do not exist. Possible signs of an agency relationship include

- government involvement in the person's activities;
- agreements and prior dealings with the person;
- instructions to the person;
- knowledge of the person's activities; and
- compensation.[47]

Agency Found. In *State v. Hageman,* the police agreed to recommend a lighter sentence for Johnson, whom they had caught attempting

---

to undercover officer, and informant repeatedly asked defendant to take possession of cocaine; trial court erred in failing to instruct on entrapment); State v. Bradshaw, 12 N.C. App. 510, 183 S.E.2d 787 (1971) (informant repeatedly asked defendant to sell him drugs and defendant only made sale when informant mentioned that undercover officer had gun; trial court erred in failing to instruct on entrapment).

45. United States v. Hollingsworth, 27 F.3d 1196, 1203 (7th Cir. 1994) (en banc); *see also* State v. Jackson, 243 N.C. 216, 220, 90 S.E.2d 507, 510 (1955) ("it is not entrapment that one has been induced by some other than a person acting for the government or state"); *Whisnant,* 36 N.C. App. at 254, 243 S.E.2d at 396 (entrapment is defense only when person who induces defendant to act is officer or agent of government). A defendant who acts under the compulsion of a person who is not a government agent still may be able to rely on a necessity or duress defense. *See* United States v. Manzella, 791 F.2d 1263, 1269 (7th Cir. 1986) (so noting). Those defenses are beyond the scope of this book.

46. *See, e.g.,* State v. Hageman, 307 N.C. 1, 28–29, 296 S.E.2d 433, 449 (1982) (entrapment defense available when "there are acts of persuasion, trickery or fraud carried out by law enforcement officers or their agents").

47. *See generally* MARCUS, *supra* note 14, § 8.03, at 324–32 (discussing factors).

19

to sell stolen property, if Johnson would try to sell stolen property to the defendant. At the direction of the police, Johnson wore a microphone and transmitter into the defendant's place of business and offered to sell the defendant stolen property. The court found that Johnson "was clearly acting as an agent of the law enforcement officers."[48]

In *State v. Caldwell,* the police discussed with an informant the possibility of his joining the Ku Klux Klan, paid his initiation fees to join the group, and told him about a reward for any information on dynamiting activities. From the money left after paying the initiation fees, the informant furnished money to the defendants to buy dynamite and assisted them in fashioning a bomb. The informant later notified the police of the defendants' plan to bomb a school, and the defendants were charged with conspiracy and attempt to bomb a school building. The court recognized that the informant was acting as a government agent, expressing concern that the police, through its agent, had played such an active role in the events. It let the guilty verdicts stand, however, finding that the question of entrapment was for the jury to resolve.[49]

Agency Not Found. In *State v. Jackson,* the defendant offered evidence that Huntley induced the defendant to write a check for $8,260, knowing that the defendant did not have the funds to cover the check. The defendant claimed that Huntley's purpose was to prosecute the defendant for writing a worthless check. The court found that "Huntley had no connection with the State" in obtaining the check from the defendant and therefore was not acting as its agent.[50]

In *State v. Thomas,* Diggs advised the police that the defendants were planning to burglarize Farrell's home. The full extent of the arrangement between Diggs and the police was that Diggs said he would let the police know when Farrell's house was going to be broken into. The court found that this evidence fell short of showing that Diggs was acting as an agent of the police.[51]

---

48. 307 N.C. 1, 4–5, 28–29, 296 S.E.2d 433, 436, 449 (1982) (finding agency but rejecting argument that defendant was entitled to dismissal as matter of law).

49. 249 N.C. 56, 60, 105 S.E.2d 189, 192 (1958); *see also* Sherman v. United States, 356 U.S. 369, 373–75 (1958) (private person was active government informant and was government agent as matter of law); State v. Sanders, 95 N.C. App. 56, 60, 381 S.E.2d 827, 830 (1989) (undercover officer testified that informant was working under direction of law-enforcement officers and was being paid his expenses; court held that informant "clearly was an agent of law enforcement" and ordered new trial for failure to instruct on entrapment); *Bradshaw,* 12 N.C. App. 510, 183 S.E.2d 787 (officer testified that he had been acting in close conjunction with informant on case for about three weeks, including times when informant contacted defendant; trial court erred in failing to instruct on entrapment).

50. 243 N.C. 216, 220, 90 S.E.2d 507, 510–11 (1955) (trial court did not err in refusing to give instructions on entrapment).

51. 52 N.C. App. 186, 202–03, 278 S.E.2d 535, 546 (1981) (trial court did not err in denying instructions on entrapment); *see also* State v. Harris, 21 N.C. App. 697, 699–700,

(c) Unwitting Intermediaries

The previous discussion assumes that the private person who is acting on the government's behalf knows that his or her principal is a law enforcement officer or other government official. Suppose, however, that the private person is an "unwitting middleman," acting at the behest of an officer but unaware of the officer's identity.

Jurisdictions are divided over how to deal with this problem, which arises in two contexts. The first involves the entrapped middleman. All jurisdictions seem to agree that a defendant may not claim entrapment based merely on a showing that the middleman was the victim of government entrapment. Traditional standing rules bar a defendant from obtaining relief for a violation of someone else's rights.[52] Jurisdictions differ, however, on whether a defendant may claim entrapment when the government entraps the middleman and the middleman in turn entraps the defendant—a situation sometimes called derivative or vicarious entrapment.[53] For example, suppose an undercover officer offers lavish inducements to Smith to engage in drug smuggling, an offense that Smith was not predisposed to commit, and Smith offers similar inducements to the defendant to persuade him to participate. In that instance, the issue is not whether the rights of Smith, the unwitting middleman, were violated but rather whether the government, acting through Smith, induced the defendant to commit an offense that he or she was not predisposed to commit.

A second, somewhat different situation involves an unwitting intermediary who, although not entrapped by the government, is still acting at the government's behest. For example, suppose undercover officers enlist a person to buy drugs for them and, because of the person's prior dealings in the drug trade, he or she is predisposed to make such purchases. May a defendant who sells drugs to the unwitting intermediary claim entrapment if the defendant was not predisposed to engage in that activity and was induced to do so by the intermediary? Courts have

---

205 S.E.2d 336, 338 (1974) (person bought marijuana from defendant and after consuming most of it informed law enforcement officer of purchase; although officer reimbursed person for his expenses, there was no evidence that officer engaged person to make buy); *cf.* State v. Clemmons, 100 N.C. App. 286, 293, 396 S.E.2d 616, 619 (1990) (trial court did not err in refusing to give instruction on bias of undercover agents and informants because informant was not in employ of or paid by police; however, opinion suggests that informant was sufficiently associated with government for defendant to rely on entrapment defense based on informant's actions).

52. *See generally* Marcus, *supra* note 14, §§ 8.02–.03, at 320–32.

53. *See, e.g.,* United States v. Hollingsworth, 27 F.3d 1196, 1203–05 (7th Cir. 1994) (Posner, C. J., writing for majority of en banc court, recognizes derivative entrapment, citing authority from some circuits; one of dissenting opinions argues that there must be direct government communication with the defendant); Annotation, *Right of Criminal Defendant to Raise Entrapment Defense Based on Having Dealt with Other Party Who Was Entrapped*, 15 A.L.R.5th 39 (1993) (discussing responses of different jurisdictions).

found in some circumstances that the defendant may claim entrapment based on the intermediary's actions.[54]

North Carolina has not definitively ruled on either of these questions. In *State v. Jackson*, the North Carolina Supreme Court stated generally that the defendant's acts may be "incited *directly or indirectly* by officers or agents of the government," but the court did not analyze the matter further.[55] In *State v. McGee,* the court found the defendant's claim of derivative entrapment meritless. There, however, the defendant appeared to argue only that he should be acquitted because the middleman had been entrapped; the defendant made no showing that the middleman induced him to commit a crime that he was not predisposed to commit.[56] In *State v. Whisnant,* the defendant's evidence showed that an undercover officer approached Reynolds and asked her to find some drugs for him and, unaware of the officer's identity, Reynolds approached the defendant about providing drugs to the officer. The court found that this evidence showed some inducement of the defendant by Reynolds as an agent of the officer and that the trial judge should have instructed the jury that entrapment is available as a defense if an officer or officer's agent induces the defendant to act.[57]

State v. Luster contains the most extensive discussion of the problem of the unwitting intermediary, but it is far from definitive. There, law enforcement officers set up an undercover fencing operation and purchased several stolen cars from Burnette. Unaware of the officers' involvement, Burnette in turn recruited the defendant to assist in locating stolen cars to sell to the fencing operation. In instructing the jury on entrapment, the trial court stated that any inducement had to come from a law enforcement officer. The trial court did not instruct that the inducement could come through someone acting as an agent for the officers, such as Burnette. A majority of the North Carolina Supreme Court found that the trial court did not err in its instructions, questioning whether an agency relationship could exist when the agent is unaware of the principal's identity. Ultimately, however, the court did not reject the possibility that an unwitting middleman could be an agent for the government and found only that the evidence was insufficient to show that the officers had made Burnette their

---

54. *See* Note, *Entrapment Through Unsuspecting Middlemen,* 95 HARV. L. REV. 1122 (1982). The author reviews the responses of various jurisdictions to this problem and finds that courts first assess whether the government has enlisted the unwitting middleman to induce a particular defendant to commit a crime. If so, the author concludes, the courts have uniformly found that the intermediary is a mere conduit for the government's solicitation and that the ultimate target of the investigation may rely on an entrapment defense. If the government does not target a particular defendant, the courts consider such factors as the control that the government exercised over the middleman's actions and the foreseeability that the middleman would induce others to join the criminal venture. *See also* authorities cited *supra* note 53.

55. 243 N.C. at 220, 90 S.E.2d at 510 (emphasis added).

56. 60 N.C. App. 658, 664–65, 299 S.E.2d 796, 800 (1983).

57. 36 N.C. App. 252, 254, 243 S.E.2d 395, 396–97 (1978).

agent for the purpose of inducing others to sell stolen cars. Recognizing the limits of the majority opinion, the dissent in *Luster* suggested that, upon a proper showing, North Carolina law would permit an entrapment defense based on inducements by an unwitting agent of the government.[58]

§ 2.5 WHAT CONSTITUTES PREDISPOSITION?

(a) Generally

The second prong of the entrapment defense in North Carolina is a lack of predisposition on the part of the defendant to commit the crime. The defendant's predisposition has been characterized as "the central inquiry" under the subjective test of entrapment.[59]

North Carolina courts have used different language to describe the predisposition element. For example, the courts have said that a defendant satisfies the element when "the criminal design originated in the minds of the government officials, rather than with the innocent defendant, such that the crime is the product of the creative activity of the law enforcement authorities."[60] Echoing this theme, the courts have said that "a line must be drawn between the trap for the unwary innocent and the trap for the unwary criminal."[61] However phrased, the inquiry boils down to essentially the same thing—whether the defendant was predisposed to commit the crime before the government approached him or her.

What sorts of things show predisposition or lack of predisposition? There is no precise measure, but the decisions identify several relevant factors, discussed in the next section. The decisions arise in a variety of procedural contexts, most often when the courts determine the admissibility of evidence offered by the state or defendant on the issue of predisposition and when they determine whether the defendant has presented sufficient evidence to warrant instructions to the jury on entrapment or dismissal of the charges altogether.[62]

---

58. 306 N.C. 566, 571–74, 588–90, 295 S.E.2d 421, 424–26, 433–34 (1982).

59. *Luster*, 306 N.C. at 575, 295 S.E.2d at 426; State v. Salame, 24 N.C. App. 1, 10, 210 S.E.2d 77, 83 (1974).

60. State v. Walker, 295 N.C. 510, 513, 246 S.E.2d 748, 749–50 (1978); *accord* State v. Sanders, 95 N.C. App. 56, 60, 381 S.E.2d 827, 830 (1989).

61. State v. Stanley, 288 N.C. 19, 30–31, 215 S.E.2d 589, 596 (1975); *see also* State v. Hageman, 307 N.C. 1, 28, 296 S.E.2d 433, 449 (1982) (persuasion, trickery, fraud, or deception must have been "practiced upon one who entertained no prior criminal intent"); State v. Burnette, 242 N.C. 164, 169, 87 S.E.2d 191, 194–95 (1955) (stating similar principles).

62. Readers interested in the admissibility of different categories of evidence should consult Chapter 5, "Evidentiary Issues," although some evidentiary problems are noted in this chapter. For the standard for issuing instructions, *see infra* § 6.2(b) (standard for issuing instructions); for nonsuit, *see infra* § 6.2(c).

Decisions involving instruction requests reveal what might seem at first to be an anomalous result. Although predisposition has been characterized as the central inquiry under the subjective test of entrapment, it has not been the focus in cases in which the North Carolina courts have denied instructions on entrapment. Generally, when the courts have refused to instruct on entrapment, the reason given has been insufficient evidence of inducement or insufficient evidence of inducement and lack of predisposition. Far rarer are decisions denying instructions solely on the basis of insufficient evidence of lack of predisposition.

This result is explainable in part by the factual nature of the inquiry into predisposition, which, like other mental states, is ordinarily for the jury to determine.[63] The result in instruction cases also shows the interrelationship between inducement and lack of predisposition. When the evidence shows some inducement by the government, that evidence also tends to support the defendant's claim that he or she would not have committed the offense in the absence of the inducement.

(b) Relevant Factors

Although predisposition is determined from the totality of circumstances, certain recurring factors can be identified.

Initiation of Discussion of Crime. The North Carolina courts have stated generally that to satisfy the predisposition element the defendant must show that the criminal design originated with the government.[64] Accordingly, evidence that the government initially suggested the offense is necessarily relevant to the issue of predisposition.[65]

Strength of Inducement. Also significant is the strength of the inducement by the government. As one court put it, "[t]he greater the inducement, the weaker the inference that in yielding to it the defendant demonstrated that he was predisposed to commit the crime in question."[66]

---

63. *See generally* MARCUS, *supra* note 14, § 4.10, at 130. The court is not precluded from finding that the evidence establishes predisposition or lack of predisposition as a matter of law. In some cases, courts have dismissed charges on entrapment grounds, taking the issue of predisposition away from the jury. *See infra* § 6.2(c) note 31 and accompanying text.

64. *See supra* § 2.4(a) note 60 and accompanying text.

65. *See Sanders*, 95 N.C. App. at 60, 381 S.E.2d at 830 (government, through informant, initiated discussion of criminal activity, which tends to show that criminal design originated with informant, not defendant; defendant was entitled to instruction on entrapment but trial court's failure to instruct, to which defendant did not object, was not plain error).

66. United States v. Hollingsworth, 27 F.3d 1196, 1199–1200 (7th Cir. 1994) (en banc). *See also* United States v. Navarro, 737 F.2d 625, 635 (7th Cir. 1984) (listing nature of inducement as one of key factors in evaluating predisposition); Paul Marcus, *Presenting, Back from the [Almost] Dead, the Entrapment Defense*, 47 FLA. L. REV. 205, 219–20 (1995) (undue involvement by government may constitute entrapment even where defendant appeared willing to commit crime).

Response to Inducement. In assessing predisposition, the courts have often inquired into whether the defendant was reluctant or willing to engage in the proposed criminal activity. Reluctance tends to defeat predisposition, while ready compliance tends to show it.[67] Even if willingness is shown, other factors may indicate that the defendant was not predisposed to commit the crime. For example, if a government agent works himself or herself into the defendant's confidence before suggesting criminal activity, the defendant's willingness to engage in the crime may have less significance.[68] Likewise, the inducement may be sufficiently strong to cause an otherwise law-abiding person to agree to the proposed criminal scheme.[69]

Ability to Comply. In addition to inquiring into whether the defendant readily agreed to the criminal activity, courts have assessed whether the defendant was readily able to engage in the activity. If the defendant was not in a position to commit the offense in the absence of the government's involvement—for example, in a drug transaction, the government agent had to assist the defendant in locating a source—this fact tends to show lack of predisposition.[70]

Some federal courts have found that the ability to engage in the proposed crime is crucial to predisposition. In *United States v. Hollingsworth,* the Seventh Circuit found that the defendant had been entrapped as a matter of law, observing:

> Predisposition is not a purely mental state, the state of being willing to swallow the government's bait. It has positional as well as dispositional force. . . . The defendant must be so situated by reason of previous training or experience or occupation

---

67. *See* State v. Hageman, 307 N.C. 1, 31, 296 S.E.2d 433, 450 (1982) ("[p]redisposition may be shown by a defendant's ready compliance, acquiescence in, or willingness to cooperate in the criminal plan where the police merely afford the defendant an opportunity to commit the crime"); State v. Jamerson, 64 N.C. App. 301, 303, 307 S.E.2d 436, 437 (1983) (evidence of defendant's initial refusals to engage in criminal conduct lent support to request for entrapment instruction); Kent v. State, 704 So. 2d 121, 125 (Fla. Dist. Ct. App. 1997) (defendant's initial refusals to sell cocaine to undercover officers were relevant to lack of predisposition).

68. *See infra* notes 84–87 and accompanying text (predisposition is measured as of time of government's initial contact with defendant, not as of time government proposed crime).

69. *See supra* note 66 and accompanying text (nature of government's inducement bears on inquiry into predisposition); *see also infra* § 5.4 (discussing use of expert testimony to show defendant's susceptibility to inducement).

70. *Compare* State v. Stanley, 288 N.C. 19, 21–24, 215 S.E.2d 589, 590–93 (1975) (court finds that defendant was entrapped as matter of law where, among other things, defendant couldn't find sources readily, defendant didn't know whether he was buying LSD or imitation, undercover officer provided transportation and supplied money, and defendant had no experience with hard drugs, only with marijuana) *with* State v. Luster, 306 N.C. 566, 575, 295 S.E.2d 421, 426 (1982) (court finds ample evidence that defendant was predisposed to commit larceny of automobile, noting among other things that defendant bragged that he dealt in stolen cars, had inside contacts at car dealership, and could get better and more expensive cars).

or acquaintances that it is likely that if the government had not induced him to commit the crime some criminal would have done so. . . .[71]

The possibility that predisposition contains a positional component—sometimes referred to as positional predisposition or positional readiness—has its roots in the Supreme Court's most recent entrapment decision, *Jacobson v. United States*. There, the Court overturned the defendant's conviction, stating that the defendant, "if left to his own devices, likely would have never run afoul of the law."[72] Although the Court did not explicitly redefine the traditional definition of predisposition under the subjective test of entrapment, its finding of entrapment as a matter of law has led some courts to scrutinize more closely whether the defendant would have committed the charged offense in the absence of the government's conduct.[73]

The North Carolina courts have not specifically addressed the concept of "positional predisposition," or the impact of *Jacobson* generally, but under North Carolina case law the ability to comply is certainly a factor in evaluating predisposition.[74]

Prior Acts. A defendant's prior crimes or other bad acts are frequently offered by the prosecution to show the defendant's predisposition to engage in the charged offense. Not all prior crimes or bad acts are admissible, however. To be admissible, they must be relevant to the defendant's predisposition to engage in the crime charged, not in criminal activity in general, and must satisfy applicable evidentiary rules.[75] Just as prior bad acts may be used to show predisposition, prior "good" acts may be admissible to show lack of predisposition.[76]

---

71. *Hollingsworth*, 27 F.3d at 1200.

72. 503 U.S. 540, 553–54 (1992).

73. In addition to *Hollingsworth, supra* note 71, *see* United States v. Knox, 112 F.3d 802, 806–10 (5th Cir. 1997) (approving positional predisposition analysis), *rev'd sub nom. on other grounds*, United States v. Brace, 145 F.3d 247 (5th Cir. 1998) (en banc) (finding that issue of positional predisposition was not preserved for appeal and declining to rule on merits of argument); *see also* United States v. Gendron, 18 F.3d 955, 962–63 (1st Cir. 1994) (Breyer, J.) (in construing *Jacobson*, court did not discuss concept of positional predisposition but did hold that predisposition turns on "how the defendant likely would have reacted to an ordinary opportunity to commit the crime," one that lacked those special features that made the government's conduct an inducement); Marcus, *supra* note 66, at 219–220 (*Jacobson* requires more searching review of government conduct); *but see* United States v. Thickstun, 110 F.3d 1394, 1397–98 (9th Cir. 1997) (rejecting positional predisposition as requirement and finding that *Jacobson* did not modify traditional test of entrapment).

74. *See supra* note 70.

75. *See infra* § 5.1(a) (discussing N.C. Rule of Evidence 404(b), which allows evidence of prior bad acts in some circumstances); § 5.1(b) (discussing relevancy restrictions); § 5.1(c) (discussing hearsay restrictions).

76. *See infra* § 5.1(d).

Although often admissible, a defendant's prior bad acts do not preclude reliance on an entrapment defense. In some cases, courts have found entrapment as a matter of law and have dismissed the charges notwithstanding evidence that the defendant had been involved in criminal activity in the past.[77]

Reputation. Courts have often stated that the defendant's reputation is a factor in determining predisposition. Reputation evidence raises thorny evidentiary questions, however, and is admissible in entrapment and other criminal cases in limited circumstances.[78]

Reasonable Suspicion. Is the presence or absence of reasonable suspicion for the government's investigation of the defendant relevant in an entrapment case? Although both the defense and prosecution have sought to use such evidence to their advantage, ordinarily it is not relevant.

The defense has argued that the government must have reasonable suspicion of criminal activity by the defendant before undertaking an undercover operation; otherwise, the defendant should be considered entrapped as a matter of law. Most jurisdictions have rejected this argument, viewing a law enforcement officer's grounds for initiating an investigation as irrelevant to the issue of whether the defendant was predisposed to commit the crime.[79] As a practical matter, however, if the government has no information about the defendant's prior activities, it may have a more difficult time responding to the defendant's claim that he or she was not predisposed to commit the offense before the government initiated its investigation.[80]

Also problematic are prosecution efforts to show that the government had reasonable suspicion to investigate the defendant. The issue has arisen in cases in which the prosecution has sought to introduce

77. *See, e.g.,* Sherman v. United States, 356 U.S. 369, 375–76 (1958) (defendant was entrapped as matter of law into selling narcotics; defendant's prior convictions for possession and sale of narcotics did not show predisposition); State v. Stanley, 288 N.C. 19, 32–33, 215 S.E.2d 589, 598 (1975) (defendant entitled to nonsuit; prior conviction for possession of marijuana did not show predisposition to possess or distribute LSD).

78. *See infra* § 5.2.

79. *See* Marcus, *supra* note 14, § 8.04 (collecting cases); United States v. Jones, 976 F.2d 176, 182 (4th Cir. 1992) (so holding); State v. Hageman, 307 N.C. 1, 31, 296 S.E.2d 433, 450 (1982) (suggesting that reasonable suspicion not required to rebut entrapment defense); *but see* Shrader v. State, 706 P.2d 834, 835–36 (Nev. 1985) ("when the police target a specific individual for an undercover operation, they must have reasonable cause to believe that the individual is predisposed to commit the crime"), *overruled,* Foster v. State, 13 P.3d 61 (Nev. 2000) (overruling *Shrader*).

80. *See infra* § 2.5(c) (predisposition is measured as of time of government's initial contact with defendant). Lack of reasonable suspicion may be a factor in evaluating whether the government's investigation of the defendant was so outrageous as to violate Due Process, but most jurisdictions have been unwilling to find that the absence of reasonable suspicion automatically violates Due Process. *See* Marcus, *supra* note 14, § 8.04; 2 LaFave et al., *supra* note 24, § 5.4(c), at 433. For discussion of the principles governing a Due Process defense based on outrageous government conduct, *see infra* § 3.3.

hearsay testimony about the defendant's prior criminal activities. For example, suppose in a case involving a charge of sale of cocaine a law enforcement officer seeks to testify that an informant told the officer that the defendant had sold cocaine to the informant on other occasions. If offered for its truth—namely, to show that the defendant sold cocaine previously and therefore was predisposed to make the charged sale—the testimony is inadmissible hearsay. The prosecution has sometimes sought to avoid this result by arguing that the testimony may be received for a purpose other than the establishment of its truth—namely, to show that the government had reasonable suspicion to investigate the defendant. The problem, however, is that the presence (or absence) of reasonable suspicion is ordinarily irrelevant in an entrapment case, so the testimony is ordinarily inadmissible for that purpose as well.[81]

Financial Interest. Other factors also may bear on predisposition, such as whether the defendant engaged in the criminal activity for profit. Lack of financial interest has been cited as tending to negate predisposition.[82] Having a financial interest does not necessarily preclude reliance on an entrapment defense, however, and in some cases the financial incentives offered by the government were found to have been part of what induced the defendant to act in the first place.[83]

(c) Timing of Government Contact

When should a defendant's predisposition be measured? At the time the government initially contacts him or her or when the government actually solicits the commission of the crime? In cases in which the solicitation to commit the crime follows soon after the initial contact, the distinction may not be very significant. In some instances,

---

81. Evidence of prior sales is not necessarily barred in a drug prosecution. The prosecution may call an informant to testify about prior sales by the defendant in the informant's presence, which would not necessarily run afoul of hearsay restrictions. *See infra* § 5.1(b) (discussing admissibility of similar prior acts by defendant). In some circumstances, the prosecution may also be able to offer otherwise inadmissible hearsay about prior sales. *See infra* § 5.1(c) (government's reasons for initiating investigation may be admissible notwithstanding hearsay restrictions if defendant opens door; also, testimony that otherwise constitutes hearsay may be admissible under North Carolina law for limited purpose of corroborating other testimony).

82. *See Stanley*, 288 N.C. at 24, 215 S.E.2d at 593 (in finding entrapment as matter of law, court noted that defendant bought drugs as favor for government agent); State v. Duncan, 75 N.C. App. 38, 46–47, 330 S.E.2d 481, 487–88 (1985) (lack of financial gain from transactions, along with other factors, supported request for instructions, but because evidence was in conflict it did not require nonsuit); United States v. Navarro, 737 F.2d 625, 635 (7th Cir. 1984) (identifying this factor as bearing on predisposition; *but cf.* State v. Thompson, 142 N.C. App. __, 543 S.E.2d 160 (2001) (taking no profit from drug sale does not necessarily establish entrapment).

83. *See, e.g.,* State v. Jamerson, 64 N.C. App. 301, 307 S.E.2d 436 (1983) (in case in which government agent paid defendant to make drug purchase for him, court finds

however, government agents may seek over time to work their way into a defendant's confidence. Timing then becomes vital.

The United States Supreme Court addressed this issue in its 1992 decision of *Jacobson v. United States.*[84] There, the defendant was the target of repeated government mailings over a twenty-six-month period. When the government eventually solicited the defendant to purchase child pornography, he ordered a magazine from a catalog previously sent to him by the government. The defendant was charged and convicted of the federal offense of knowingly receiving child pornography through the mails.

The Court overturned the conviction, holding that the evidence was insufficient to allow the jury to find that the defendant was predisposed to commit the offense prior to the government's investigation. The Court discounted the defendant's willingness to order pornography when eventually solicited by the government, stating that "[t]he evidence that the [defendant] was ready and willing to commit the offense came only after the Government had devoted 2 1/2 years to convincing him that he had or should have the right to engage in the very behavior proscribed by law."[85]

The impact of this approach is that a defendant's predisposition must be measured as of the time the government initially approaches the defendant, not when it actually solicits the defendant to commit an offense. Further, ready acquiescence to the government's solicitation may not be that significant if the solicitation occurs some time after the initial government contact.[86]

There appear to be no reported decisions in North Carolina directly addressing the issue presented in *Jacobson,* but North Carolina courts likely would follow the Supreme Court's lead. The Court's reasoning in *Jacobson* appears to effectuate the traditional purpose of the entrapment defense in North Carolina—namely, to preclude conviction when the defendant's acts are the product of the creative activity of law enforcement authorities. The North Carolina Supreme Court implicitly endorsed this approach in a decision that preceded *Jacobson,* finding entrapment as a matter of law in a case in which over time an undercover

---

that defendant was entitled to instruction on entrapment); State v. Blackwell, 67 N.C. App. 432, 313 S.E.2d 797 (1984) (although defendant made no profit from transactions, defendant bought drugs for undercover officer because officer indicated that he could get defendant a job; defendant entitled to instruction on entrapment); United States v. Hollingsworth, 27 F.3d 1196 (7th Cir. 1994) (in case in which government agent paid defendant fee for money laundering, court finds entrapment as matter of law and dismisses charges).

84. 503 U.S. 540 (1992).

85. *Id.* at 553.

86. *Jacobson* also has sparked discussion among courts about the meaning of predisposition itself, not just the issue of when predisposition should be measured. *See supra* § 2.5(b) notes 71–73 and accompanying text.

officer ingratiated himself into the defendant's confidence and then solicited the defendant to purchase drugs. The court found that the criminal design originated with the officer and that, notwithstanding the defendant's willingness to purchase drugs once asked to do so by the officer, there was no evidence that the defendant was predisposed to commit the offense.[87]

---

87. *See Stanley,* 288 N.C. 19, 215 S.E.2d 589.

3   Related Defenses

§ 3.1 WANT OF ELEMENT 33
  (a) Generally 33
  (b) Crimes Involving Lack of Consent 34
  (c) Conspiracy 35
  (d) Stolen Goods 36
  (e) Drug Offenses 37

§ 3.2 RELIANCE DEFENSES 38
  (a) Entrapment by Estoppel 38
  (b) Public Authority 39
  (c) Innocent Intent 40

§ 3.3 OUTRAGEOUS GOVERNMENT CONDUCT 40
  (a) Generally 40
  (b) Procedure for Raising 42

§ 3.4 SENTENCING ENTRAPMENT 44

3 Related Defenses

Several defenses are closely related to entrapment. Although sometimes confused with entrapment, these defenses have their own requirements, which are the subject of this chapter.

§ 3.1 WANT OF ELEMENT

(a) Generally

Sometimes those who set out to catch a person in the act of committing a crime do so in such a way as to make the person's act not criminal at all. For example, suppose a property owner, in the hope of catching a person in the act of stealing, encourages that person to "steal" the owner's property. Because the owner has willingly parted with the property, the taking is treated as having occurred with the owner's consent, and because the crime of larceny requires a taking without the owner's consent, no larceny will have taken place.[1]

These kinds of cases resemble entrapment cases because they involve the setting of a trap. The legal theory in such cases is distinct from entrapment principles, however.[2] The central issue under this theory is whether the prosecution has proven beyond a reasonable doubt all of the elements of the crime charged—a burden the prosecution must bear in all criminal cases. If the prosecution fails to meet its burden, the defendant must be acquitted regardless of whether he or she meets the requirements for entrapment or any other defense.

Discussed below are several cases that, although involving different offenses, all address the same general problem of whether the person setting a trap did so in such a way as to defeat a required element of the offense and thus preclude conviction.[3]

---

1. *See generally* ROLLIN M. PERKINS & RONALD N. BOYCE, CRIMINAL LAW 1161 (3d ed. 1982).

2. *See* State v. Booher, 305 N.C. 554, 562, 290 S.E.2d 561, 565 (1982) (principle "is not the same as, and should not be confused with, the doctrine of entrapment"); *see also* Sorrells v. United States, 287 U.S. 435, 442–43 (1932) (recognizing distinction between want-of-element defense and entrapment).

3. *See also infra* § 3.2(c) (discussing "innocent intent" defense, a form of want-of-element defense).

(b) Crimes Involving Lack of Consent

For some offenses, consent by the victim is a complete defense. If the purported victim consents to the defendant's act—or, more precisely, the prosecution fails to prove that the act occurred without the victim's consent—the defendant is not guilty of the offense.

In trap cases, the courts have placed an additional gloss on the meaning of consent. The victim is deemed to have consented to the act if the victim "arranges for a crime to be committed against himself and aids, encourages or solicits the commission of it."[4] In these circumstances, the defendant's actions are "not against the will" of the purported victim; hence, the defendant has not committed the offense.[5]

Trap cases in which consent may be at issue include:

- physical and sexual assaults;[6]
- larcenies;[7] and
- burglaries and other break-ins.[8]

A consent defense has inherent limitations. Consent is not a defense, of course, to the many offenses that do not recognize consent as a basis for acquittal.[9] Thus although the victim's consent would bar a conviction of assault, which requires proof of a nonconsensual touching or threat

---

4. *Booher*, 305 N.C. at 561, 290 S.E.2d at 564.

5. State v. Hughes, 208 N.C. 542, 552, 181 S.E. 737, 743–44 (1935).

6. *See Booher*, 305 N.C. at 562–64, 290 S.E.2d at 565–66 (evidence not sufficient to support conviction of first-degree sexual offense because victim induced defendant to force victim into engaging in homosexual act); State v. Burnette, 242 N.C. 164, 87 S.E.2d 191 (1955) (evidence sufficient to support conviction of assault with intent to commit rape; victim did not consent to defendant's attack by merely meeting defendant at place demanded by defendant); State v. Nelson, 232 N.C. 602, 61 S.E.2d 626 (1950) (in prosecution for assault, trial court erred in excluding evidence that woman lured defendant into putting his hands on her, which supported defendant's theory that prosecution did not prove lack of consent to touching).

7. *See Hughes*, 208 N.C. 542, 181 S.E. 737; State v. Smith, 152 N.C. 798, 799, 67 S.E. 508, 509 (1910) (recognizing that larceny does not occur when "conduct of the owner amounts to a consent that his property may be taken"); State v. Adams, 115 N.C. 775, 782, 20 S.E. 722, 722 (1894) (trial court erred by not specifically instructing jury that larceny cannot be committed when owner consents to taking, though purpose may have been to apprehend defendant); State v. Jernagan, 4 N.C. 483 (1817); *see also* D. E. Ytreberg, Annotation, *Larceny: Entrapment or Consent*, 10 A.L.R.3d 1121 (1966).

8. *See Hughes*, 208 N.C. 542, 181 S.E. 737 (recognizing consent as possible defense to felonious breaking and entering of store but finding that store employee did not consent to entry and in any event had no authority, express or implied, to consent to entry); State v. Goffney, 157 N.C. 624, 73 S.E. 162 (1911) (evidence was insufficient to support conviction of breaking and entering because owner's agent, at owner's instance, induced defendant to break into store), *cited with approval in* State v. Boone, 297 N.C. 652, 656–57, 256 S.E.2d 683, 685–86 (1979); *see also* Judy E. Zelin, Annotation, *Maintainability of Burglary Charge, where Entry into Building Is Made with Consent*, 58 A.L.R.4th 335 (1987).

9. *See Booher*, 305 N.C. at 562, 290 S.E.2d at 565 (consent may not serve as defense when want of consent is not required for conviction); State v. Coleman, 270 N.C. 357, 363, 154 S.E.2d 485, 489–90 (1967) (to same effect); *see also* 1 Wayne R. LaFave &

of force,[10] it would not bar a conviction of homicide, which is unlawful regardless of whether the victim consents.[11]

Even in the case of offenses that require lack of consent for conviction, merely allowing a crime to go forward does not amount to consent. For example, a person may wait quietly in his or her store, knowing that the defendant intends to break in, without being deemed to have consented to the break-in. But if the person sends an employee to induce the defendant to break in, such an action would amount to consent and would require acquittal.[12]

Some cases suggest that if the criminal intent originates with the defendant, consent is not a basis for acquittal.[13] Such an approach, however, appears to confuse entrapment with consent. The defendant's predisposition would seem to be irrelevant if the victim consents to the act, and other North Carolina cases support this view.[14]

(c) Conspiracy

A person is guilty of conspiracy if (1) he or she agrees with another person to commit an unlawful act *and* (2) both persons intend to carry out the agreement. In light of this definition, a conspiracy cannot exist when the defendant and an undercover officer are the only parties to the agreement. In that instance, only the defendant truly intends to carry out the agreement; the officer is merely feigning the intent to commit a crime.[15]

AUSTIN W. SCOTT, JR., SUBSTANTIVE CRIMINAL LAW § 5.10, at 687–91 (1986) (finding that consent may serve as defense when it either negates element of offense or precludes infliction of harm to be prevented by law defining offense); 1 PAUL H. ROBINSON, CRIMINAL LAW DEFENSES § 66, at 307–19 (1984) (similar discussion).

10. See *Nelson*, 232 N.C. 602, 61 S.E.2d 626; *see also* State v. Gooding, 196 N.C. 710, 146 S.E. 806 (1929) (crime of battery consists of physical violence or constraint inflicted on another without consent); *but cf.* 1 LAFAVE & SCOTT, *supra* note 9, § 5.10, at 688 (consent is defense to battery only if bodily harm is not serious).

11. See State v. Forrest, 321 N.C. 186, 362 S.E.2d 252 (1987) (jury could find defendant guilty of first-degree murder for mercy killing); *see also* Anne Dellinger, *How We Die in North Carolina*, POPULAR GOV'T, Spring 1999, at 5–6 (discussing difference between assisted suicide, which is generally considered legal, and mercy killing).

12. *Booher*, 305 N.C. at 561, 290 S.E.2d at 565 ("if a person knows a crime is contemplated against his person or property, he may wait passively and permit matters to go on, or create the conditions under which the crime against himself may be committed, for the purpose of apprehending the criminal without being held to have assented to the act").

13. See State v. Burnette, 242 N.C. 164, 174–75, 87 S.E.2d 191, 198–99 (1955) (upholding instructions to that effect).

14. See *Booher*, 305 N.C. at 562, 290 S.E.2d at 565; State v. Hughes, 208 N.C. 542, 181 S.E. 737 (1935); State v. Adams, 115 N.C. 775, 20 S.E. 722 (1894) (error to instruct jury that if defendant had previous intent to steal, he would be guilty of larceny even if owner's agent had persuaded defendant to steal goods).

15. See State v. Walker, 251 N.C. 465, 475–77, 112 S.E.2d 61, 68–70 (1960); State v. Wilkins, 34 N.C. App. 392, 400, 238 S.E.2d 659, 665 (1977); United States v. Lewis, 53 F.3d 29 (4th Cir. 1995) (trial court erred in giving general instruction on conspiracy and in denying defendant's request for specific instruction that jury must acquit defendant if it found that defendant and undercover agent were the only parties to agreement).

A person may still be convicted of conspiracy if he or she enters into an agreement with an officer *and* a third person who intends to carry out the agreement. In that instance, there are at least two people who agree to the crime and intend to carry it out.[16] In addition, even when the defendant and an undercover officer are the only parties involved, the defendant may be convicted of solicitation. That crime is complete upon the defendant's solicitation of another to commit a crime, whether or not the person solicited is willing to proceed.[17]

(d) Stolen Goods

For a person to be convicted of receiving or possessing stolen goods, the property must in fact be stolen.[18] In *State v. Hageman,* the court applied this principle to an undercover fencing operation. There, the police sold the defendant previously-stolen silverware that the police had recovered. The court held that the defendant could not be convicted of receiving stolen property because, once recovered by the police, the silverware lost its status as stolen. (For the same reason, the defendant could not be convicted of possessing stolen goods.)[19]

This general principle has a number of limitations. First, the property at issue must actually be recovered by the police. If not, it retains its stolen character.[20] Second, the principle does not apply to controlled substances, which retain their illegal status regardless of whether they have been in the possession of the police.[21] Third, *Hageman* does not

---

16. *See Walker,* 251 N.C. at 475–77, 112 S.E.2d at 68–70; State v. Rosario, 93 N.C. App. 627, 637, 379 S.E.2d 434, 440 (1989); *Wilkins,* 34 N.C. App. at 400, 238 S.E.2d at 665. Of course, any other requirements for conspiracy would have to be satisfied as well. *See generally* ROBERT L. FARB, NORTH CAROLINA CRIMES: A GUIDEBOOK ON THE ELEMENTS OF CRIME 34–36 (Institute of Government, 5th ed. 2001).

17. *See* State v. Keen, 25 N.C. App. 567, 570–71, 214 S.E.2d 242, 244 (1975). Of course, any other requirements for solicitation would have to be satisfied as well. *See generally* FARB, *supra* note 16, at 33–34 (setting forth elements of solicitation to commit felony); John Rubin & Ben F. Loeb, Jr., *Punishments for North Carolina Crimes & Motor Vehicle Offenses: 2000 Cumulative Supplement,* ADMINISTRATION OF JUSTICE BULLETIN NO. 2000/04, at 4 (Institute of Government, 2000) (solicitation to commit misdemeanor may constitute crime under North Carolina law for certain misdemeanors only).

18. *See* FARB, *supra* note 16, at 204–10.

19. 307 N.C. 1, 296 S.E.2d 433 (1982); *see also* United States v. Dove, 629 F.2d 325 (4th Cir. 1980) (applying similar principle under federal law and finding that certain goods had been recovered by police and had lost their status as stolen while other goods had not been recovered).

20. The dividing line may not always be clear. In *Hageman,* an informant (Johnson) tried to surrender a ring he had stolen, but the police refused to accept it. At the direction of the police, Johnson then sold the ring (along with the silverware that had been in police custody) to the defendant. The defendant argued that the police had recovered the ring because Johnson was acting as an agent of the police and had offered to turn it over to them. While the police seemed to have control over disposition of the property, the court found that the ring retained its stolen status because the police had not actually regained possession of it. *See* 307 N.C. at 10–11, 296 S.E.2d at 439.

21. *See infra* § 3.1(e).

preclude conviction of attempting to receive stolen goods. The defendant argued in *Hageman* that because the goods had lost their stolen status, making it impossible to complete the crime of receiving stolen goods, he could not be convicted of attempting to commit that crime. The court rejected the defendant's impossibility defense, stating:

> [W]e hold that when a defendant has the specific intent to commit a crime and under the circumstances as he reasonably saw them did the acts necessary to consummate the substantive offense, but, because of facts unknown to him essential elements of the substantive offense were lacking, he may be convicted of an attempt to commit the crime.[22]

(e) Drug Offenses

Unlike stolen property, which loses its stolen character when it falls into the hands of the police, "controlled substances do not lose their status as controlled substances" when the police gain possession of them. Consequently, a person may be convicted of possession of a controlled substance even though the police provided the substance to the person.[23]

Police involvement may nevertheless limit the possible charges against the defendant. In *State v. Clark,* for example, the police intercepted a package containing more than ten pounds of marijuana, removed all but a small amount of the marijuana to make sure that it did not fall into the wrong hands, and then undertook a controlled delivery of the package to the defendant, the intended recipient. The court held that the defendant could not be convicted of possession of the original, larger amount of marijuana because he never actually possessed it. The court rejected the argument that the defendant had constructive possession of the greater amount, holding that he never exercised dominion or control over the original package.[24]

---

22. 307 N.C. at 13, 296 S.E.2d at 441; *accord* State v. Gunnings, 122 N.C. App. 294, 468 S.E.2d 613 (1996) (rejecting impossibility defense and upholding conviction of attempted possession of cocaine). The impossibility defense is beyond the scope of this book, but the cases have recognized, and the language in *Hageman* appears flexible enough to preserve, some variants of the defense. *See, e.g.,* State v. Coble, 351 N.C. 448, 527 S.E.2d 45 (2000) (finding that attempted second-degree murder is not a crime under North Carolina law because it is logically impossible for person to specifically intend to commit form of murder that does not have specific intent to kill as element); State v. Lea, 126 N.C. App. 440, 449–50, 485 S.E.2d 874, 879–80 (1997) (finding for similar reasons that attempted felony murder is not a crime); State v. Addor, 183 N.C. 687, 690, 110 S.E. 650, 651 (1922) ("where it is clear that the perpetration of the crime is impossible, and that is known to the party, there can be no indictable attempt"); 2 LaFave & Scott, *supra* note 9, § 6.3(a), at 39–50 (discussing situations in which impossibility is and is not a defense); Perkins & Boyce, *supra* note 1, at 627–35 (similar discussion).

23. State v. Rosario, 93 N.C. App. 627, 634–35, 379 S.E.2d 434, 438 (1989).

24. 137 N.C. App. 90, 93–95, 527 S.E.2d 319, 321–22 (2000).

The court in *Clark* upheld the defendant's conviction of conspiracy to traffic in the larger amount, however, finding sufficient evidence that the defendant and the sender of the package were working together. The court also noted that attempted possession of the larger amount would be an appropriate charge.[25]

§ 3.2 RELIANCE DEFENSES

Like the entrapment defense, the defenses discussed in this section involve some sort of dealings between the government and defendant. Unlike cases involving entrapment, however, a defendant asserting each of the following defenses knew that he or she was dealing with the government and acted in reliance on that relationship.

(a) Entrapment by Estoppel

One type of reliance defense arises when the defendant commits what would otherwise be an illegal act in reasonable reliance on representations by the government that his or her conduct is legal. For example, in *Cox v. Louisiana*, the police informed the defendants that they could demonstrate across the street from a courthouse but then arrested them for violating a state statute prohibiting demonstrations near courthouses. The U.S. Supreme Court found that the state had engaged in an "indefensible sort of entrapment" and that Due Process prohibited conviction of the defendants.[26]

This defense has come to be known as *entrapment by estoppel*,[27] but the term is somewhat misleading because the defendant need not satisfy the standard requirements for entrapment. To establish entrapment by estoppel, the defendant need not show that the government official used trickery, fraud, or some other device to induce the defendant to act; indeed, the official may have unintentionally misled the defendant about the legality of the conduct in question.[28] The require-

---

25. *See also* State v. Gunnings, 122 N.C. App. 294, 468 S.E.2d 613 (1996) (defendant sought to buy cocaine from undercover officer, and officer sold her a counterfeit substance; relying on *Hageman*, discussed *supra* § 3.1(d) and note 22, court rejects defendant's impossibility defense and upholds conviction for attempted possession of cocaine).

26. 379 U.S. 559, 571 (1965) (vacating conviction on Due Process grounds); *see also* Raley v. Ohio, 360 U.S. 423, 437–39 (1959) (applying similar analysis in vacating conviction). Although the defense is rooted in Due Process principles, it is distinct from the Due Process defense of outrageous conduct, discussed *infra* § 3.3.

27. *See* United States v. Aquino-Chacon, 109 F.3d 936, 938–39 (4th Cir. 1997) (recognizing defense but finding that it did not warrant dismissal on evidence presented); United States v. Achter, 52 F.3d 753, 755 (8th Cir. 1995) (to same effect); United States v. Baptista-Rodriguez, 17 F.3d 1354, 1368 n.18 (11th Cir. 1994) (recognizing theory).

28. *See* Fred Warren Bennett, *From* Sorrells *to* Jacobson: *Reflections on Six Decades of Entrapment Law, and Related Defenses, in Federal Court*, 27 WAKE FOREST L. REV. 829, 862 (1992).

ments of the defense are not easy to meet, however—the defendant must have "acted in a reasonable fashion, relying on clear directions by a government official."[29]

(b) Public Authority

A second type of reliance defense—sometimes referred to as *public authority*—arises when the defendant commits what would otherwise be an illegal act on behalf of law enforcement or other government officials. In *State v. Tillman,* for example, the defendant presented evidence that he was acting as an informant for the police when he purchased heroin. The North Carolina Court of Appeals ordered a new trial because the trial court failed to instruct the jury to acquit the defendant if it found that he had been acting as an agent of law enforcement.[30]

Tillman relied on Section 90-101(c)(5) of the North Carolina General Statutes, which expressly allows law enforcement officers and agents to possess controlled substances if acting within the course and scope of their duties. The public authority defense would appear to be available, however, regardless of the existence of a specific statute. Courts have recognized as a general rule that a person acting on behalf of law enforcement officers may not be prosecuted for acts that the officers may lawfully undertake.[31]

---

29. PAUL MARCUS, THE ENTRAPMENT DEFENSE § 1.16, at 49 (2d ed. 1995) (synthesizing recent federal cases and finding that defendants have had a difficult time meeting requirements of defense); *see also* Jeffrey F. Ghent, Annotation, *Criminal Law: "Official Statement" Mistake of Law Defense,* 89 A.L.R.4th 1026 (1991) (collecting cases). Although the question is not settled, it appears that the defense is decided by the jury, not by the judge, when the facts are in dispute. *See* United States v. West Indies Transp., Inc., 127 F.3d 299, 313–14 (3d Cir. 1997) (assessing whether evidence was sufficient to warrant jury instruction on entrapment by estoppel and finding evidence insufficient); United States v. Abcasis, 45 F.3d 39 (2d Cir. 1995) (finding evidence sufficient to warrant instruction); *but see* Sean Connelly, *Bad Advice: The Entrapment by Estoppel Doctrine in Criminal Law,* 48 U. MIAMI L. REV. 627, 640–42 (1994) (arguing that defense should be decided by judge, as in cases involving Due Process defense of outrageous conduct, discussed *infra* § 3.3(b), but recognizing that a number of cases indicate that defense involves jury question).

30. 36 N.C. App. 141, 242 S.E.2d 898 (1978) (standard instruction on entrapment inadequate to communicate defendant's theory of defense to jury). In an earlier case, the court of appeals rejected the defendant's proposed instruction on agency. *See* State v. Wilkins, 34 N.C. App. 392, 400–401, 238 S.E.2d 659, 665 (1977). That decision was issued before *Tillman,* however, and the court there rejected the instruction for, among other reasons, the defendant's failure to point to any authority for the instruction.

31. *See* United States v. Achter, 52 F.3d 753, 755 (8th Cir. 1995) (distinguishing entrapment by estoppel and public authority defenses and holding that latter defense is available when defendant reasonably relies on authority of government official to engage him or her in covert activity); *Baptista-Rodriguez,* 17 F.3d at 1368 n.18 (noting that "actions properly sanctioned by the government are not illegal"); United States v. Mason, 902 F.2d 1434, 1438–41 (9th Cir. 1990) (defense available to person who reasonably believes that he or she was acting as agent of law enforcement even if belief was mistaken); *see also* N.C. GEN. STAT. 15A-405 (protecting private person who assists law enforcement officer in effecting arrest or preventing escape). For a discussion of public authority principles, *see generally* 2 ROBINSON, *supra* note 9, §§ 142, 149.

(c) Innocent Intent

A third reliance defense, sometimes called an *innocent intent* defense, arises when the defendant commits what otherwise would be an illegal act in the honest belief that he was performing the act in cooperation with the government. This defense is a form of want-of-element, or negating, defense. The evidence of the defendant's innocent intent negates the mental state required for conviction and precludes the prosecution from proving beyond a reasonable doubt all the elements of the offense.[32] For example, in *State v. Allison,* the defendant was acting as an informant for the police when he accompanied another person who was planning to rob a convenience store. The North Carolina Supreme Court held that the evidence was insufficient to support the defendant's conviction of attempted robbery. The assistance rendered by the defendant to the police showed that he intended for the police to foil the robbery, negating the intent to rob, a required element of the offense.[33]

§ 3.3 OUTRAGEOUS GOVERNMENT CONDUCT

(a) Generally

A defense sometimes raised along with or in lieu of an entrapment defense is the Due Process defense of outrageous government conduct—that is, that the government's conduct was so outrageous that Due Process bars prosecution of the defendant. This defense is independent of the entrapment defense and may be raised regardless of whether the defendant meets the traditional requirements of entrapment. While a great deal has been written about the outrageous-conduct defense, in practice it rarely succeeds.

The defense springs from the United States Supreme Court's 1973 opinion in *United States v. Russell.* Although the Court in *Russell* found no Due Process violation on the evidence presented, it acknowledged that dismissal may be warranted in some circumstances:

> [W]e may some day be presented with a situation in which the conduct of law enforcement agents is so outrageous that due process principles would absolutely bar the government from invoking judicial processes to obtain a conviction. . . .[34]

32. For a discussion of other want-of-element defenses, *see supra* § 3.1.

33. 319 N.C. 92, 352 S.E.2d 420 (1987) (trial court erred in denying motion to dismiss; conviction vacated); *see also Baptista-Rodriguez,* 17 F.3d at 1368 n.18 (distinguishing this theory from entrapment by estoppel and public authority); *Mason,* 902 F.2d at 1438–41 (ordering new trial for trial court's failure to give specific instructions to jury explaining this theory of acquittal).

34. 411 U.S. 423, 431–32 (1973). While a Due Process defense is often seen in cases involving an entrapment defense, it is not limited to that context and may bar prosecution

Subsequently, in 1976 in *Hampton v. United States,* a majority of the Supreme Court reaffirmed that Due Process could warrant dismissal on the right set of facts, although the Court again found such relief unwarranted on the evidence presented.[35]

Based on the authority of *Russell* and *Hampton,* most courts have recognized the defense of outrageous government conduct.[36] State courts have held that such conduct may warrant dismissal under state constitutional guarantees as well.[37] Courts also may have the inherent supervisory power to dismiss a prosecution for outrageous government conduct.[38]

In contrast to the subjective test of entrapment, the defendant's predisposition to commit the crime is not determinative under this defense. Rather, the inquiry turns on whether the government's conduct meets some standard of outrageousness. In essence, the government must engage in extraordinary or shocking misconduct, a standard that has proven difficult for defendants to meet. Few federal decisions have found a Due Process violation, prompting the Fourth Circuit to observe that the federal courts have demonstrated a "high shock threshold" even in the presence of extremely unsavory government conduct.[39] The Due Process

---

whenever government activity violates fundamental fairness. *See* 2 WAYNE R. LAFAVE ET AL., CRIMINAL PROCEDURE § 5.4(c), at 429–30 n.29 (2d ed. 1999); *see also supra* § 3.2(a) (discussing defense of entrapment by estoppel, which is also based on Due Process concerns).

35. 425 U.S. 484 (1976). In *Hampton,* a three-justice plurality issued the opinion of the Court, with two justices concurring, three dissenting, and one abstaining. Although the three-justice plurality sought to disavow *Russell,* the five justices who concurred and dissented comprised a majority of the court, and they accepted that a defendant could raise a Due Process claim based on outrageous government conduct.

36. *See* MARCUS, *supra* note 29, § 7.05, at 274–75; Tim A. Thomas, Annotation, *What Conduct of Federal Law Enforcement Authorities in Inducing or Cooperating in Criminal Offenses Raises Due Process Defense Distinct from Entrapment,* 97 A.L.R. FED. 273 (1990). Some circuits have refused to recognize the Due Process defense. *See, e.g.,* United States v. Boyd, 55 F.3d 239, 241 (7th Cir. 1995) (holding that defense does not exist in that circuit); United States v. Tucker, 28 F.3d 1420 (6th Cir. 1994) (divided panel refuses to recognize defense); *but see* Stephen A. Miller, Comment, *The Case for Preserving the Outrageous Government Conduct Defense,* 91 NW. U. L. REV. 305 (1996) (criticizing such decisions).

37. *See* MARCUS, *supra* note 29, § 7.11, at 310–17; *see also* Danny R. Veilleux, Annotation, *Actions by State Officials Involving Defendant as Constituting "Outrageous" Conduct Violating Due Process Guaranties,* 18 A.L.R.5th 1 (1994).

38. *See Hampton,* 425 U.S. at 495 (concurring opinion notes this authority); Bennett, *supra* note 28, at 860–61 (citing cases recognizing this authority and concluding that, as in cases involving a Due Process claim, only flagrant misconduct by the government would support dismissal).

39. United States v. Osborne, 935 F.2d 32, 36 (4th Cir. 1991); *see also* United States v. Twigg, 588 F.2d 373 (3d Cir. 1978) (early, often distinguished, decision finding that nature and extent of police involvement was so overreaching that it barred prosecution of defendants for their part in illegal manufacture of controlled substance); 2 LAFAVE, ET AL., *supra* note 34, § 5.4(c), at 431–32 (LaFave concludes that instances of government conduct outrageous enough to violate Due Process have been exceedingly rare, but finds that some types of government conduct may still support Due Process defense, such as inducing violence or threat of violence against innocent parties, exploiting a sexual relationship to bring about a crime, or offering extraordinarily large financial inducements).

defense seems to have fared somewhat better in state court prosecutions, although the defendant still has a difficult burden to meet.[40]

How has this defense fared in North Carolina? The North Carolina courts appear to recognize that a defendant may raise a Due Process defense, but in the few cases in which the issue has been raised the courts found that relief was not warranted. In two decisions, the court of appeals acknowledged *Russell* and the Due Process principles it expressed but found that the evidence presented did not show a Due Process violation.[41]

A North Carolina case from the 1950s, decided well before *Russell,* also lends support to the viability of a Due Process defense in an appropriate case. In *State v. Caldwell,* a police informant took an active part in a plan by the Ku Klux Klan, of which the defendants were members, to bomb a school. The defendants' evidence indicated that the informant made two trips to Charlotte to pick up dynamite, paid for the dynamite with money that the police had provided him, assisted in fashioning the dynamite into a bomb, and carried the bomb to the school in his car. The North Carolina Supreme Court expressed strong disapproval of the role that the police department, through its agent, had played in the bombing plans. But, recognizing that the evidence of the informant's involvement was in conflict, the court accepted the jury's finding that the defendants were the ones who originated the bomb plan and that they had merely accepted the informant's assistance.[42]

(b) Procedure for Raising

How does a defendant raise the defense of outrageous conduct in violation of Due Process? Many courts have found that the defense

---

40. *See* State v. Glosson, 462 So. 2d 1082, 1084–85 (Fla. 1985) (comparing state and federal cases); *see also* State v. Lively, 921 P.2d 1035 (Wash. 1996) (finding Due Process violation where informant attended AA/NA meetings for purpose of luring recovering addicts into committing illegal acts and then struck up and exploited romantic relationship with defendant, a recovering alcoholic with no criminal history); Metcalf v. State, 635 So. 2d 11 (Fla. 1994) (illegal manufacture of crack cocaine by police for use in reverse-sting operation violated Due Process); People v. Shine, 590 N.Y.S.2d 965 (N.Y. App. Div. 1992) (finding Due Process violation where undercover officers showed up at defendant's home in middle of night and demanded drugs while displaying weapon).

41. *See* State v. Rosario, 93 N.C. App. 627, 635–37, 379 S.E.2d 434, 439 (1989) (police intercepted drug courier, seized cocaine, repackaged approximately same amount of cocaine, and directed courier to deliver new package to defendant; government's conduct was not outrageous); State v. Salame, 24 N.C. App. 1, 7–8, 210 S.E.2d 77, 81–82 (1974) (government did nothing other than inquire of defendant whether he had drugs for sale and arrange a meeting at which sale could be made; government's conduct was not outrageous).

42. 249 N.C. 56, 60, 105 S.E.2d 189, 192 (1958); *see also* 2 LaFave et al., *supra* note 34, § 5.4(a), at 431–32 (suggesting that government conduct that induces others to engage in violence or threat of violence against innocent parties may support Due Process defense).

presents a question of law, to be decided by the judge, not the jury.[43] Consequently, a defendant may move before trial to dismiss the charges on Due Process grounds. Indeed, under federal criminal procedure, a defendant risks waiver if he or she fails to raise the defense before trial.[44] Under North Carolina criminal procedure, a defendant may, but apparently is not required to, make the motion before trial.[45]

Courts have sometimes held an evidentiary hearing before trial to address a defendant's motion to dismiss on Due Process grounds.[46] Courts also have deferred ruling on such motions until after trial.[47] Because the outrageous-conduct defense is viewed as one involving a question of law, the judge would determine disputed issues of fact at either stage of the proceedings. This approach contrasts with cases involving an entrapment defense, in which disputed issues of fact are for the jury to resolve and rarely, if ever, could a court rule on the defense before trial.[48]

If the court denies a pretrial motion to dismiss based on Due Process grounds and the defendant then pleads guilty instead of proceeding to trial, the defendant may lose the right to appeal the adverse ruling.[49] Under the federal rules of criminal procedure, a defendant may, with the consent of the court and prosecutor, enter a conditional

---

43. *See, e.g.,* United States v. Stanley, 765 F.2d 1224, 1232 (5th Cir. 1985) (no error to refuse to submit issue to jury for decision); United States v. Quinn, 543 F.2d 640, 648 (8th Cir. 1976) (to same effect); Commonwealth v. Monteagudo, 693 N.E.2d 1381, 1383 (Mass. 1998) (to same effect).

44. *See, e.g.,* United States v. Pitt, 193 F.3d 751, 760–61 (3d Cir. 1999) (finding that motion must be made before trial because Federal Rule of Criminal Procedure 12(b) requires that defenses based on defect in instigation of prosecution be raised before trial; for good cause court may excuse failure to make pretrial motion); United States v. Duncan, 896 F.2d 271, 274–75 (7th Cir. 1990) (motion must be made before trial; if defendant fails to raise defense at all, appellate review is for plain error only).

45. *See* N.C. Gen. Stat. 15A-952 (any defense capable of being determined without trial may be raised by pretrial motion; certain motions, but apparently not a motion to dismiss on Due Process grounds, must be made before trial); *cf. Salame,* 24 N.C. App. at 6, 210 S.E.2d at 81 (defendant moved to dismiss on Due Process grounds before trial and at close of state's evidence; court did not specifically address procedure for making such a motion).

46. *See, e.g.,* United States v. Batres-Santolino, 521 F. Supp. 744 (N.D. Cal. 1981) (granting dismissal after pretrial evidentiary hearing).

47. *See, e.g.,* United States v. Williams, 644 F.2d 950, 952–53 (2d Cir. 1981) (finding that trial court did not err in deferring ruling on motion until end of trial); *cf.* N.C. Gen. Stat. 15A-952(f) (granting court discretion on when to rule on pretrial motion).

48. *See supra* § 2.1 notes 14–16 and accompanying text (subjective test of entrapment involves jury issues). One of the principal rationales for deferring decision on a motion raising a Due Process defense is that the defense is often intertwined with evidence of entrapment to be decided by the jury. Defendants face some risk, however, if they press certain Due Process issues at trial. *See infra* § 5.1(c) (by challenging government's reasons for launching investigation, defendant may open door to otherwise inadmissible hearsay).

49. *See* United States v. Montilla, 870 F.2d 549 (9th Cir. 1989) (by pleading guilty, defendant waived outrageous government conduct claim), *amended on other grounds,* 907 F.2d 115 (9th Cir. 1990); *see also* 5 La Fave et al., *supra* note 34, § 21.6(a), at 222–32

guilty plea and reserve the right to appeal adverse pretrial rulings.[50] North Carolina does not have a similar rule or statute.[51] If the case is properly before the appellate court, the question of a Due Process violation is reviewed de novo, although the trial court's findings of fact are entitled to deference.[52]

§ 3.4 SENTENCING ENTRAPMENT

Sentencing entrapment is a relatively new doctrine, appearing primarily in the federal courts. In essence, defendants have claimed that although they may have been predisposed to commit certain offenses, they committed more serious ones only at the government's urging. The doctrine has two variations. One is similar to the traditional, subjective version of the entrapment defense, with the essential inquiry being whether the defendant was predisposed to commit the more serious offense. The second variation rests on Due Process principles, challenging as outrageous the particular methods employed by the government in soliciting the more serious offense.[53]

Sentencing entrapment has been raised most often in federal drug prosecutions. For example, at sentencing, defendants have claimed that undercover officers or informants convinced them to buy or sell far greater quantities of controlled substances than they initially intended

---

(discussing generally rights waived by guilty plea). Generally, a defendant does not have the right to an immediate appeal of an interlocutory order, such as the denial of a pretrial motion to dismiss on Due Process grounds, but in limited circumstances may be able to obtain appellate review by petition for writ of certiorari. *See* N.C. R. APP. P. 21(a)(1). The state's right to appeal the dismissal of charges is governed by N.C. GEN. STAT. 15A-1445, which allows the state to appeal only if double jeopardy principles would not bar retrial of the defendant. *See also* United States v. Scott, 437 U.S. 82 (1978) (stating general rule); State v. Vestal, 131 N.C. App. 756, 509 S.E.2d 249 (1998) (double jeopardy barred appeal by state).

50. *See* FED. R. CRIM. P. 11(a)(2).

51. *Cf.* N.C. GEN. STAT. 15A-979(b) (defendant may plead guilty and appeal denial of suppression motion if defendant gives timely notice of this intent). A defendant who has pled guilty may be able to obtain review of pretrial rulings by writ of certiorari, but review is discretionary. *See* N.C. GEN. STAT. 15A-1444(e) (appellate review after guilty plea).

52. *See* Bennett, *supra* note 28, at 862 (discussing federal cases addressing standard of review for Due Process defense); *see also* Ornelas v. United States, 517 U.S. 690 (1996) (ultimate question of reasonable suspicion to stop and probable cause under Fourth Amendment must be reviewed de novo on appeal, although trial court's findings of fact are reviewed for clear error only); State v. Parker, 137 N.C. App. 590, 594, 598, 530 S.E.2d 297, 300, 302 (2000) (questions of law are reviewed de novo, while underlying findings of fact are binding if supported by competent evidence).

53. The Fourth Circuit refers to the first type of claim, which is based on traditional entrapment notions, as *sentencing entrapment* and to the second, which is based on Due Process principles, as *sentencing manipulation,* but courts do not use these labels uniformly. *See* United States v. Jones, 18 F.3d 1145, 1153 (4th Cir. 1994) (distinguishing between the two doctrines but declining to rule on validity of either).

to buy or sell. Consequently, defendants argue, the court should not consider these tainted transactions in calculating the appropriate sentence under federal sentencing guidelines.[54] A number of federal courts have accepted the doctrine, although some have yet to take a position or have refused to recognize it.[55]

Because of the way offenses are structured in North Carolina, the sentencing entrapment doctrine may encounter less resistance in this state than it might in federal court. Under current North Carolina law, the doctrine could potentially serve as a conventional affirmative defense rather than as an argument at sentencing. For example, suppose that a person tries to sell a small amount of marijuana to an undercover officer—a low-level felony in North Carolina—and the officer induces the person to sell a far greater quantity—enough to charge the person with trafficking in marijuana, a separate offense with a far greater punishment. If the evidence shows that the defendant was not predisposed to sell the larger amount, entrapment could be a basis for acquittal of the more serious trafficking charge. In such a case, if the defendant presents sufficient evidence of entrapment, the jury would consider the defense at the close of the evidence as in other entrapment cases.[56] At

---

54. *See* United States v. Stauffer, 38 F.3d 1103 (9th Cir. 1994) (finding sentencing entrapment and ordering resentencing where government induced defendant to sell greater amount than he would have sold); United States v. Barth, 990 F.2d 422 (8th Cir. 1993) (recognizing doctrine but finding that government's repeated buys from defendant, which increased potential punishment, did not amount to sentencing entrapment). The argument may arise in non-drug cases as well. *See* United States v. Cannon, 886 F. Supp. 705, 708–09 (D.N.D. 1995) (finding sentencing entrapment and manipulation where government induced defendant to obtain machine gun, which carried much stiffer sentence), *rev'd on other grounds,* 88 F.3d 1495, 1503 (8th Cir. 1996).

55. *See generally* United States v. Stavig, 80 F.3d 1241, 1245 n.3 (8th Cir. 1996) (reviewing decisions of circuit courts). Some of the decisions rejecting the doctrine have rejected certain variants only. *See, e.g.,* United States v. Garcia, 79 F.3d 74 (7th Cir. 1996) (rejecting Due Process variant of doctrine). Defendants prosecuted federally may have less of a need to use this doctrine at sentencing in light of the United States Supreme Court's decision in *Apprendi v. New Jersey,* 530 U.S. 466 (2000), which held that any fact other than a prior conviction that increases the punishment beyond the prescribed statutory maximum must be submitted to the jury and proven beyond a reasonable doubt. Under *Apprendi,* factors that have been decided by federal judges at sentencing, such as the quantity of drugs, may have to be submitted to the jury as part of the definition of the offense. *See, e.g.,* United States v. Angle, 230 F.3d 113, 121–24 (4th Cir. 2000) (drug quantities that could expose defendants to punishment greater than statutory maximum must be charged in indictment, submitted to jury, and proven beyond reasonable doubt). In light of these rulings, defendants prosecuted federally may be able to raise entrapment as a conventional affirmative defense to certain offenses rather than as an argument at sentencing. *See infra* notes 56–57 and accompanying text (discussing this use of doctrine).

56. *See generally* United States v. Shephard, 4 F.3d 647, 650 (8th Cir. 1993) (defendant's argument that he was entrapped into selling crack rather than powdered cocaine, which were separate offenses, was not sentencing argument but, rather, was theory of entrapment on elements of offense; theory was therefore for jury to resolve in determining guilt or innocence). If the defendant challenges the more serious offense based on the Due Process defense of outrageous conduct, the judge rather than the jury would likely rule on the defense. *See supra* § 3.3(b) (discussing procedure for raising Due Process defense).

least one decision suggests that the North Carolina courts would be receptive to such a defense.[57]

Entrapment considerations also would appear to be relevant to sentencing determinations under North Carolina sentencing law. Under structured sentencing, which governs most criminal offenses in North Carolina, the court may consider any factors that have mitigating value. Although the existence of a mitigating factor is not a basis for reducing an offense to a lesser offense, the court may take such factors into account in determining the length of the defendant's sentence.[58]

---

57. *See* State v. Rosario, 93 N.C. App. 627, 636–37, 379 S.E.2d 434, 439 (1989) (court finds that officers' tactics were not inappropriate but notes that they could not "arbitrarily aggravate an offense by increasing the amount of drugs they supply to a defendant").

58. *See* N.C. GEN. STAT. 15A-1340.16(e) (allowing court to consider listed factors at sentencing and any other factors that have mitigating value); *see also* N.C. GEN. STAT. 15A-1340.13(g), (h) (allowing court to suspend sentence that otherwise must be activated if it finds extraordinary mitigation). A failed entrapment defense also may have mitigating value. *See generally* N.C. GEN. STAT. 15A-1340.16(e)(1) (listing as mitigating factor that defendant committed offense under compulsion that was insufficient to constitute defense but significantly reduced defendant's culpability); United States v. McClelland, 72 F.3d 717, 726 (9th Cir. 1995) (in imposing reduced sentence, trial court could properly determine that defendant who proposed illegal scheme, but who later expressed reservations and acted only after inducements by government, is less morally blameworthy and less likely to commit crimes in future than defendant who eagerly participated in illegal scheme with no inducement other than initial suggestion by government agent).

4 Procedural Issues

§ 4.1 Disclosure of Informants' Identities 49

§ 4.2 Severance of Co-Defendants 51

§ 4.3 Inconsistent Defenses 52

      (a) Generally 52

      (b) A Rule and Some Exceptions 53

      (c) Illustration 57

      (d) A Simpler Approach? 57

4   Procedural Issues

Raising an entrapment defense may have a number of procedural consequences. Some, such as the rules on obtaining disclosure of the identity of a confidential informant, may be favorable to defendants. Others, such as the inconsistent-defense doctrine, may be traps for the unwary.

§ 4.1   Disclosure of Informants' Identities

Entrapment cases often involve the use of police informants, a practice that may generate several legal complications.[1] This section considers the circumstances under which the defendant is entitled to disclosure of an informant's identity.

The United States Supreme Court announced the general standard for disclosure of informants' identities in *Roviaro v. United States.*[2] The Court recognized that the government has a limited privilege to withhold from disclosure the identity of a person who furnishes to law enforcement information about violations of the law. The purpose of the privilege is to protect the public's interest in effective law enforcement. Under the Due Process Clause of the United States Constitution and principles of fundamental fairness, however, the privilege must give way when disclosure of the informant's identity "is relevant and helpful to the defense of an accused, or is essential to a fair determination of a cause."[3]

---

1. For example, the Fourth Amendment may prohibit searches conducted by informants, while the Fifth Amendment may bar statements elicited by informants. *See generally* Robert L. Farb, Arrest, Search, and Investigation 228–29 (Institute of Government, 2d ed. 1992).

2. 353 U.S. 53 (1957).

3. *Id.* at 60–61; *see also* E. H. Schopler, Annotation, *Accused's Right to, and Prosecution's Privilege against, Disclosure of Identity of Informant*, 76 A.L.R.2d 262 (1961) (collecting cases on disclosure of informants). In some circumstances the defendant also has a right to disclosure of an informant's identity in challenging probable cause for a search or arrest. *See* N.C. Gen. Stat. 15A-978(b); McCray v. Illinois, 386 U.S. 300 (1967). The contents of an informant's communications and other information also may be discoverable. *See* N.C. Gen. Stat. 15A-903(a)(2) (statutory provisions on disclosure of defendant's statements to confidential informant); Kyles v. Whitley, 514 U.S. 419, 445–49 (1995) (government has obligation to disclose adverse information bearing on credibility of informant as part of duty to disclose exculpatory evidence); *see also Roviaro*, 353 U.S. at 60 (discussing other circumstances in which informant privilege does not apply).

Roviaro instructs that, in determining whether fundamental fairness requires disclosure, courts should use a multi-factor approach, taking into consideration the crime charged, possible defenses, potential significance of the informant's testimony, and any other relevant factors. In practice, however, courts often focus on whether the informant was a "participant" in the crime or a "mere tipster," requiring disclosure of the identity of the former but not the latter. One who takes some active part in the offense, arranges for its commission, or is otherwise a percipient or material witness may be viewed as a "participant." One who only provides an investigative lead for law enforcement personnel, in contrast, is often characterized as a "tipster."[4]

Using either the multi-factor approach or the participant/tipster distinction, courts generally have required disclosure of an informant's identity when the informant has played some role in the alleged entrapment of the defendant.[5] The defendant's mere assertion of an entrapment defense, however, does not require disclosure. In cases in which the defendant offered no evidence of entrapment, disclosure has been denied.[6]

The defendant has the burden of showing that the circumstances warrant disclosure.[7] If the defendant meets this burden, he or she is entitled to learn both the identity and whereabouts of the informant.[8]

---

4. *See generally* FARB, *supra* note 1, at 230; State v. Johnson, 81 N.C. App. 454, 344 S.E.2d 318 (1986) (requiring disclosure where informant could testify to details surrounding crime); State v. Grainger, 60 N.C. App. 188, 190, 298 S.E.2d 203, 204–05 (1982) (denying disclosure where informant neither participated in offense nor helped arrange its commission); United States v. Price, 783 F.2d 1132, 1137–39 (4th Cir. 1986) (requiring disclosure where informant set up deal).

5. *See* State v. Hodges, 51 N.C. App. 229, 275 S.E.2d 533 (1981) (informant introduced undercover officer to defendant, who sold marijuana to officer in informant's presence; disclosure required); State v. Orr, 28 N.C. App. 317, 220 S.E.2d 848 (1976) (informant helped engineer events leading up to crime; disclosure required); McLawhorn v. North Carolina, 484 F.2d 1, 4–7 (4th Cir. 1973) (informant could testify from personal knowledge to material events surrounding offense; disclosure required), *vacating on habeas* 16 N.C. App. 153, 191 S.E.2d 410 (1972); *see also* State v. Parker, 61 N.C. App. 585, 587, 301 S.E.2d 450, 451 (1983) (disclosure of informant should have been ordered but error was harmless because defendant already knew informant's identity).

6. *See, e.g.,* State v. Fletcher, 279 N.C. 85, 92–94, 181 S.E.2d 405, 411–12 (1971) (defendant presented no evidence that government induced him to commit crime); *Grainger,* 60 N.C. App. at 190–91, 298 S.E.2d at 204–05 (evidence indicated that informant was mere tipster, and disclosure was not required on mere assertion of entrapment); State v. McAuliffe, 22 N.C. App. 601, 604–05, 207 S.E.2d 1, 3 (1974) (defendant presented no evidence that informant was "participant" in crime and no evidence of entrapment).

7. *See* State v. Cheek, 351 N.C. 48, 57, 520 S.E.2d 545, 551 (1999); State v. Watson, 303 N.C. 533, 536–37, 279 S.E.2d 580, 582–83 (1981); *see also* State v. Moctezuma, 141 N.C. App. __, 539 S.E.2d 52 (2000) (reviewing procedure for hearing motions to compel disclosure and finding that trial court erred in hearing motion outside presence of defendant and defense counsel).

8. *See* State v. Brockenborough, 45 N.C. App. 121, 122, 262 S.E.2d 330, 331 (1980) (state must disclose to defendant best information available to prosecution and law enforcement concerning informant's whereabouts); *accord* State v. Logan, 79 N.C. App.

In some circumstances, the defendant may be entitled to a continuance of the trial to interview the informant and determine whether his or her testimony would be beneficial.[9] If the prosecution refuses to identify the informant, the court may dismiss the charges altogether.[10]

§ 4.2 Severance of Co-Defendants

In cases involving multiple defendants, the question may arise whether they should be tried together or separately. A defendant is entitled to a separate trial if his or her position is so antagonistic to the position taken by one or more co-defendants that the defendant would otherwise be denied a fair trial.[11] Under this standard, courts have found that severance is not necessarily required when one defendant relies on an entrapment defense and the others do not.[12] In some instances, however, such an inconsistency may pose sufficient prejudice to require severance.

In *State v. Simmons*,[13] the court concluded that a defendant who was not raising an entrapment defense was prejudiced by the trial court's failure to grant a severance. There, two defendants were charged with trafficking in marijuana. Defendant Simmons, who was relying on an entrapment defense, testified at trial that he had been pressured into committing the offense by an agent of the police. Defendant Hallman, who was not claiming entrapment, did not testify. The court of appeals held that the trial judge erred in denying Hallman's

---

420, 422, 339 S.E.2d 449, 451 (1986). Some courts have also required the government to make a reasonable effort to produce the informant for trial or for interview by the defendant. *See* United States v. Montgomery, 998 F.2d 1468, 1473 (9th Cir. 1993) (so holding as matter of fairness and citing other circuits reaching same result); *see also* State v. Newkirk, 73 N.C. App. 83, 86–88, 325 S.E.2d 518, 521 (1985) (suggesting that trial court may require state to make good faith effort to locate informant).

9. *Compare Hodges*, 51 N.C. App. at 232, 275 S.E.2d at 535 (denial of motion to continue was error, requiring new trial) *with* State v. Tate, 58 N.C. App. 494, 497–98, 294 S.E.2d 16, 18–19 (1982) (denial of motion to continue was not error), *aff'd on other grounds*, 307 N.C. 464, 298 S.E.2d 386 (1983).

10. *See* Roviaro v. United States, 353 U.S. 53, 60–61 (1957) (so holding); State v. McEachern, 114 N.C. App. 218, 441 S.E.2d 574 (1994) (dismissing charges).

11. *See* State v. Pickens, 335 N.C. 717, 725, 440 S.E.2d 552, 556–57 (1994) (discussing standard for severance based on antagonistic defenses); *see also* Wade R. Habeeb, Annotation, *Antagonistic Defenses as Ground for Separate Trials of Codefendants in Criminal Case*, 82 A.L.R.3d 245 (1978). Severance may be required on other grounds as well. *See* N.C. Gen. Stat. 15A-927(c)(2) (severance required when necessary to "a fair determination of guilt or innocence").

12. *See, e.g.*, United States v. Ricks, 882 F.2d 885, 894–95 (4th Cir. 1989) (defendant not entitled to severance from co-defendant who raised entrapment defense; alleged conflict in defenses was not so prejudicial as to preclude fair trial); United States v. Mulherin, 710 F.2d 731, 736 (11th Cir. 1983) (co-defendant's reliance on entrapment defense does not itself require severance for a defendant not asserting that defense).

13. 65 N.C. App. 294, 296–98, 309 S.E.2d 493, 495–96 (1983).

motion to sever. It found that other than the testimony of Simmons—in which he admitted engaging in the drug deal and implicated Hallman—the state's evidence against Hallman was weak. It also found that had the trials not been joined, the jury may have never heard Simmons' testimony. The court concluded in these circumstances that Hallman was denied a fair trial by being tried with Simmons.

A defendant relying on entrapment as a defense also may wish to be tried separately from a co-defendant. For example, suppose a co-defendant could corroborate the defendant's claim that he or she had been entrapped by an undercover officer but, because of the risk of self-incrimination or other tactical considerations, the co-defendant is unwilling to testify at a joint trial. If the co-defendant would testify favorably at a separate trial, severance may be required to protect the defendant's right to present exculpatory evidence.[14]

§ 4.3 INCONSISTENT DEFENSES

(a) Generally

Some jurisdictions take the position that the entrapment defense is unavailable to a defendant who denies having committed the offense, reasoning that such a defense is inconsistent with denial of the offense.[15] A defendant charged with possession of marijuana, for example, might be barred in some states from claiming entrapment if he or she denies having possessed the marijuana. This ban on "inconsistent defenses," which is peculiar to entrapment cases and generally is not applied in other contexts, has been criticized frequently and its constitutionality questioned.[16] Yet, as discussed in the next section, various incarnations persist.

---

14. *See generally* State v. Alford, 289 N.C. 372, 385–389, 222 S.E.2d 222, 231–233 (failure of trial court to sever trials deprived defendant of testimony of co-defendant, which would have corroborated defendant's alibi claim), *vacated sub nom. on other grounds,* Carter v. North Carolina, 429 U.S. 809 (1976); State v. Paige, 316 N.C. 630, 641–42, 343 S.E.2d 848, 855–56 (1986) (trial court did not err in denying severance; defendant failed to make adequate showing that co-defendant would have testified favorably at separate trial); 4 WAYNE R. LAFAVE ET AL., CRIMINAL PROCEDURE § 17.2(c), at 615–17 (1999) (potential stumbling block to motion to sever on this ground is possibility that co-defendant may remain unwilling to testify at separate trial unless he or she is tried first, something that may be difficult for moving defendant to control).

15. *See* Timothy E. Travers, Annotation, *Availability in State Court of Defense of Entrapment where Accused Denies Committing Acts which Constitute Offense Charged,* 5 A.L.R.4th 1128 (1981); *see also* Timothy E. Travers, Annotation, *Availability in Federal Court of Defense of Entrapment where Accused Denies Committing Acts which Constitute Offense Charged,* 54 A.L.R. FED. 644 (1981) (discussing approaches taken by federal courts before U.S. Supreme Court abolished doctrine in federal cases, discussed *infra* § 4.3(d)).

16. *See, e.g.,* PAUL MARCUS, THE ENTRAPMENT DEFENSE § 6.22, at 254 n.177 (2d ed. 1995) (doctrine may relieve state of burden of proving all elements of offense beyond reasonable doubt); 2 LAFAVE ET AL., *supra* note 14, § 5.3(c), at 421–22 (doctrine may force defendant to surrender presumption of innocence and privilege against self-incrimination).

May a defendant prosecuted in North Carolina rely on entrapment as a defense if he or she denies having committed the offense? The answer is maybe. There are two reasons for this uncertainty. First, although the North Carolina courts have stated generally that defendants may not rely on inconsistent defenses in entrapment cases, the specific rules are fairly technical and their application depends on the evidence in each case. Second, in its 1988 decision in *Mathews v. United States*,[17] the United States Supreme Court rejected any prohibition on inconsistent defenses in federal entrapment cases. Although not binding on state courts, the decision, like other Supreme Court decisions interpreting federal entrapment law, has considerable persuasive value, and it has caused some states to reconsider their positions. The North Carolina Supreme Court has not had the opportunity to evaluate its own inconsistent-defense doctrine in light of *Mathews*.

The remainder of this chapter reviews North Carolina's rules on inconsistent defenses in entrapment cases, discusses how those rules might apply to a simple case involving a charge of possession of marijuana, and considers the potential impact of *Mathews* in North Carolina.

(b) A Rule and Some Exceptions

State v. Neville establishes the general rule in North Carolina that, except in certain circumstances, entrapment is unavailable as a defense if the defendant denies having committed the offense charged. If the defendant denies the offense, the court may refuse to instruct the jury on entrapment.[18] To apply this doctrine correctly, several issues must be considered, and not all have settled answers.

An initial question concerns what it means to deny having committed the offense. Must the defendant affirmatively admit committing the offense to make use of an entrapment defense, or is the right to rely on entrapment lost only if the defendant denies the offense? In cases in which the defendant takes the stand, the distinction ordinarily makes little practical difference because, when asked, the defendant will have to either admit or deny. The distinction may be quite important, however, in cases in which the defendant does not testify.[19]

---

17. 485 U.S. 58 (1988).

18. 302 N.C. 623, 276 S.E.2d 373 (1981); *see also* State v. Hunt, 283 N.C. 617, 624, 197 S.E.2d 513, 518 (1973) (characterizing entrapment as a plea of "confession and avoidance," an older description of some affirmative defenses). Although the practical effect of this doctrine is to prevent the defendant from denying the offense if he or she wishes to claim entrapment, the court may not actually refuse to permit the defendant to deny the offense. Thus, if the defendant claims entrapment, the court may not bar the defendant from denying the offense; it may only reject his or her entrapment claim.

19. The distinction may also be important if the defendant takes the stand but has insufficient information to admit or deny an element of the offense. In that instance, a

As a condition of claiming entrapment, some jurisdictions have required defendants to admit the elements of the offense regardless of whether they testify—an approach that would seem to raise thorny constitutional questions.[20] Others have refused to require an affirmative admission by the defendant, holding that defendants may remain entirely silent and put the state to its proof.[21] Under the latter approach, a nontestifying defendant still might be deemed to have denied committing the offense if he or she introduces evidence contradicting the elements of the offense—a qualification that obviously complicates the inquiry further. Mere cross-examination of the state's witnesses or argument to the jury apparently would not constitute a denial, however.[22]

No North Carolina decision specifically addresses the problem, so the matter is not entirely free from doubt, but North Carolina appears to be in the "can't deny" rather than the "must admit" camp. *State v. Neville,* the lead North Carolina case on the question, appears to hold only that a defendant may not deny committing the offense if he or she wishes to claim entrapment (and some exceptions to this rule exist, discussed below).[23] In *State v. Luster,* the supreme court reiterated that the entrapment defense is not available if the defendant denies the criminal act; the court added that a defendant may rely on entrapment under a not guilty plea, thus suggesting that a defendant

---

rule concerned only with whether the defendant has denied the offense would not necessarily bar an entrapment defense.

20. *See* State v. Soule, 811 P.2d 1071 (Ariz. 1991) (defendant must admit elements of crime to claim entrapment); *but cf.* State v. Preston, 4 P.3d 1004, 1008–1011 (Ariz. Ct. App. 2000) (even though Arizona law requires defendant to admit elements of crime, trial court may not instruct jury that only issue for its consideration is whether defendant had been entrapped; such an instruction amounts to directed verdict against defendant on elements of offense and violates presumption of innocence and right to jury finding of guilt beyond reasonable doubt).

21. *See, e.g.,* United States v. Annese, 631 F.2d 1041, 1047 (1st Cir. 1980) (in pre-*Mathews* decision, court held that inconsistent-defense doctrine did not require defendant to elect between remaining silent and raising entrapment defense; "[t]o hold otherwise would raise a serious fifth amendment question").

22. *See, e.g.,* United States v. Valencia, 645 F.2d 1158, 1172 (2d Cir. 1980) (in pre-*Mathews* decision, court held that defendant was entitled to raise defense of entrapment since he did not take stand to deny his participation in transaction and did not affirmatively introduce any other evidence that he was not involved; summation by defense counsel that defendant was not involved in transaction did not preclude defendant from relying on entrapment defense); Melton v. State, 713 S.W.2d 107, 112 (Tex. Crim. App. 1986) (although defense of entrapment is not available to defendant who denies commission of offense, it is available to defendant who pleads not guilty and who does not take stand or otherwise offer any testimony inconsistent with commission of offense). The discussion here about the various approaches used at different times by different jurisdictions is not intended to be exhaustive. For a fuller review, *see* annotations cited *supra* note 15.

23. 302 N.C. at 626, 276 S.E.2d at 375.

may remain silent and put the state to its proof.[24] A decision by the court of appeals used the terms "denial" and "admission" interchangeably but ultimately found that the defendant was not entitled to entrapment instructions only for those offenses that he specifically denied committing.[25] Apparently no North Carolina decisions have refused to allow the defendant to rely on entrapment for failing to admit having committed the crime.

Assuming that the defendant denies having committed the offense within the meaning of North Carolina law, it remains to be considered whether an exception exists to the bar on raising entrapment as a defense. There are two, probably three, such exceptions under North Carolina law.

First, if the state's evidence raises the issue of entrapment, the defendant has the right to rely on entrapment while denying the elements of the crime. In that situation, the courts view any inconsistency as having been created by the state, not by the defendant.[26]

Second, a defendant has the right to rely on entrapment while denying the intent element of a crime and perhaps other mental elements required for conviction. *Neville* held that the denial of criminal intent is not inconsistent with the entrapment defense because a defendant claiming entrapment is essentially claiming that he or she did not entertain a criminal intent.[27] Since the issuance of the *Neville* opinion, the question has arisen whether a defendant may deny other mental elements, such as knowledge, and still rely on entrapment. In *Luster,* the defendant claimed entrapment in response to a charge of larceny of a stolen vehicle and also denied knowing that the vehicle was stolen. The

---

24. 306 N.C. 566, 581 n.4, 295 S.E.2d 421, 429 n.4 (1982).

25. *See* State v. Sanders, 95 N.C. App. 56, 61–63, 381 S.E.2d 827, 830–31 (1989). Other North Carolina decisions have found insufficient evidence of entrapment in cases in which the defendant denied committing the crime. Although the decisions were not concerned with whether inconsistent defenses were permissible in entrapment cases, they are in accord with the idea that North Carolina law only bars a defendant from relying on entrapment if he or she denies having committed the crime. *See* State v. Swaney, 277 N.C. 602, 609, 178 S.E.2d 399, 403 (1971) (defendant claimed that he knew nothing about crime and did not participate in it; question of entrapment therefore did not arise); State v. Boles, 246 N.C. 83, 85, 97 S.E.2d 476, 477–78 (1957) (to same effect).

26. *See Neville,* 302 N.C. at 626, 206 S.E.2d at 375 (recognizing this exception). Without addressing this exception specifically, some cases have examined the state's evidence to determine whether it raised a question of entrapment. *See Boles,* 246 N.C. 83, 97 S.E.2d 476 (defendant denied being present during offense or participating in it; court reviews state's evidence to determine whether it raised entrapment defense); State v. Braun, 31 N.C. App. 101, 102–03, 228 S.E.2d 466, 467 (1976) (state's evidence disclosing entrapment was sufficient to require submission of entrapment question to jury but not to warrant dismissal; defendant presented no evidence).

27. 302 N.C. at 626, 206 S.E.2d at 375. Older cases suggesting the contrary no longer appear to be good law. *See, e.g.,* State v. Yost, 9 N.C. App. 671, 673, 177 S.E.2d 320, 321 (1970) (court upheld denial of entrapment instructions in burglary case in which defendant denied having any criminal intent in entering house).

supreme court declined to rule on the issue of whether entrapment was available as a defense in these circumstances.[28] In a later case, however, the court of appeals found that a defendant could deny knowing that the substance he was selling was cocaine and still claim that he was entrapped into selling the substance.[29]

The rationale for these two exceptions is that the defendant has not taken inconsistent positions and so may rely on entrapment. A third, more general exception is that the defendant may rely on entrapment whenever there is no inherent inconsistency between the defendant's entrapment claim and his or her denial of certain elements of the crime.[30] North Carolina decisions do not explicitly discuss this exception but nevertheless appear to recognize its viability, allowing defendants in some cases to assert entrapment along with a want-of-element defense. For example, in a case involving a charge of receiving stolen goods, the defendant argued both that the goods had lost their character as "stolen" (because the police had regained possession of them before providing them to the defendant) and that the police had entrapped him into receiving the goods. The supreme court expressed no concern about the presentation of both defenses.[31]

This third exception can be difficult to apply consistently. In *Neville,* for example, the defendant was charged with possession of LSD with intent to sell and sale of LSD. The defendant's version was that an undercover agent offered the defendant $20 to pretend to get LSD for the agent, who then would provide it to a third person. The defendant admitted that he participated in a scheme intended to make it look like he was selling LSD, but he denied ever possessing the LSD (claiming that the agent had maintained possession of it at all times) and denied making a real sale. The supreme court held that it was inconsistent for the defendant to deny committing the acts with which he was charged—possession and sale of LSD—and also claim that the

---

28. 306 N.C. at 581 n.4, 295 S.E.2d at 429 n.4.

29. *Sanders,* 95 N.C. App. at 61–62, 381 S.E.2d at 830–31; *see also Luster,* 306 N.C. at 592, 295 S.E.2d at 435 (Exum, J., dissenting, finds that denying knowledge that vehicles were stolen does not render entrapment defense unavailable to defendant).

30. *See* MARCUS, *supra* note 16, § 6.25, at 261–63 (entrapment is normally allowed when there is no true conflict or inconsistency); 2 LaFAVE ET AL., *supra* note 14, § 5.3(c), at 422–23 (even under traditional inconsistent-defense doctrine, defendant may raise defense of entrapment when there is no inherent inconsistency between defense and denial of particular acts).

31. *See* State v. Hageman, 307 N.C. 1, 296 S.E.2d 433 (1982); *see also* State v. Burnette, 242 N.C. 164, 87 S.E.2d 191 (1955) (in case where lack of consent was element of offense, defendant claimed that he was entrapped and also that victim consented); State v. Rosario, 93 N.C. App. 627, 379 S.E.2d 434 (1989) (defendant who was charged with conspiracy claimed that he was entrapped and that there was no agreement). Other cases involving want-of-element claims are discussed *supra* § 3.1; *see also* Stripling v. State, 349 So. 2d 187, 191 (Fla. Dist. Ct. App. 1977) (defendant may deny being party to conspiracy and raise issue that any overt acts were result of entrapment; defenses are not necessarily inconsistent).

agent had entrapped him. One could plausibly argue, however, as did the dissent in the court of appeals, that there was no fundamental inconsistency between an entrapment defense and the defendant's claim that the agent induced him to commit acts that could result in conviction for possession and sale of LSD.[32]

(c) Illustration

How would the North Carolina rules discussed above apply in a relatively uncomplicated case involving a charge of possession of marijuana? A defendant who testifies and admits possessing the marijuana certainly could claim entrapment. So, apparently, could a defendant who does not testify, although as a practical matter the failure to testify would weaken any entrapment claim. In either instance, the defendant could argue that the state had failed to prove the elements of the offense beyond a reasonable doubt and still claim entrapment. For example, the defendant could argue that the prosecution had failed to prove that the substance recovered by law enforcement officers was, in fact, marijuana.

What is less clear is the extent to which entrapment is available as a defense in North Carolina if the defendant affirmatively introduces evidence, through his or her own testimony or via the testimony of other defense witnesses, contradicting the elements of the offense. The exception to the inconsistent-defense bar that is easiest to apply in this scenario is the one permitting the defendant to present evidence contradicting the mental elements of the offense. Thus, without losing the right to claim entrapment, the defendant could testify or introduce other evidence to the effect that he or she did not know that the substance involved was marijuana.

The applicability of other exceptions is less certain. If the state's evidence raises an issue of entrapment, the defendant can introduce affirmative evidence contradicting any of the elements of the offense and still claim entrapment. But the defendant would not be sure that this option is available until the state rests, and even then he or she could not proceed safely unless the trial court indicated at that stage that the state's evidence had raised an entrapment issue.

Under the general exception for defenses that are not inherently inconsistent with entrapment, the defendant might be able to introduce evidence contradicting some or all of the elements of the offense without losing the right to claim entrapment. Because of the difficulty of forecasting how a court might apply this exception, however, the outcome of this strategy is uncertain.

(d) A Simpler Approach?

The federal courts struggled with the problem of inconsistent defenses before 1988, coming up with various and conflicting solutions.

---

32. 49 N.C. App. 684, 687, 272 S.E.2d 164, 166–67 (1980) (dissenting opinion).

In its 1988 decision in *Mathews v. United States,* the United States Supreme Court laid the controversy to rest, at least in federal cases.[33] The Court held that a defendant could rely on entrapment while taking other positions, including denying the acts underlying the offense. The Court recognized that the criminal law has always allowed defendants to take inconsistent positions and saw nothing unique about cases involving the entrapment defense. The Court also recognized that the ability to raise inconsistent defenses is subject to a practical constraint—namely, that defendants who present inconsistent testimony or take inconsistent positions may irreparably damage their credibility before the jury and undermine their chances of acquittal.

The Court did not address whether the United States Constitution required this result, instead rejecting the inconsistent-defense bar as a matter of federal law. The decision therefore is not binding on state courts.[34] The Court's reasoning has persuasive value, however, and a number of state courts have altered their rules in light of *Mathews.*[35] It has been suggested that North Carolina should reconsider its position as well.[36] Such a change would make North Carolina entrapment law consistent with its general criminal law, which ordinarily permits defendants to rely on alternative, conflicting defenses.[37] It would no doubt simplify the trial of entrapment cases as well. Until the North Carolina Supreme Court changes course, however, defendants seeking to rely on an entrapment defense and trial courts considering whether to instruct on it will have to brave the uncertain currents of the inconsistent-defense doctrine.

---

33. 485 U.S. 58, 59 & n.1 (1988) (noting inconsistency across circuits); *see also* Timothy E. Travers, Annotation, *Availability in Federal Court of Defense of Entrapment where Accused Denies Committing Acts which Constitute Offense Charged,* 54 A.L.R. FED. 644 (1981) (reviewing cases before *Mathews*).

34. Although not specifically dealt with in *Mathews,* constitutional issues still may be present. *See supra* § 4.3(a) notes 16, 20; *but see* Eaglin v. Welborn, 57 F.3d 496 (7th Cir. 1995) (en banc) (in post-*Mathews* decision, court finds that although a state rule limiting presentation of defenses could violate Due Process in some instances, inconsistent-defense doctrine used by Illinois in entrapment cases did not present constitutional issue), *rev'g* 815 F. Supp. 1181 (C.D. Ill. 1993) (finding that inconsistent-defense doctrine violated Fifth and Sixth amendments).

35. *See* Hopson v. State, 625 So. 2d 395, 400 (Miss. 1993) (abolishing inconsistent-defense ban in light of *Mathews*); MARCUS, *supra* note 16, § 6.22, at 254 & n.175 (citing additional cases that have so held).

36. *See* George Robert Hicks, III, Note, 11 CAMPBELL L. REV. 279 (1989); *but see* Karis A. Hastings, Note, *Entrapment and Denial of the Crime: A Defense of the Inconsistency Rule,* 1986 DUKE L. J. 866 (1986) (defending inconsistent-defense rule before issuance of *Mathews* opinion).

37. *See, e.g.,* State v. Todd, 264 N.C. 524, 530, 142 S.E.2d 154, 159 (1965) ("'The defendant's plea of not guilty entitled him to present evidence that he acted in self-defense, that the shooting was accidental, or both. Election is not required. The defendant may rely on more than one defense.'"), *quoting* State v. Wagoner, 249 N.C. 637, 639, 107 S.E.2d 83, 85 (1959).

5   Evidentiary Issues

§ 5.1   PRIOR BAD ACTS 61

    (a)   Generally 61

    (b)   Relevancy Restrictions 63

    (c)   Hearsay Restrictions 66

    (d)   Prior Good Acts 68

§ 5.2   REPUTATION EVIDENCE 69

§ 5.3   CONVERSATIONS WITH OFFICERS
     AND INFORMANTS 72

§ 5.4   EXPERT TESTIMONY 72

5   Evidentiary Issues

§ 5.1   Prior Bad Acts

(a)   Generally

The courts have often stated that under the subjective test of entrapment the critical inquiry is whether the defendant was predisposed to commit the crime.[1] A recognized way for the prosecution to show predisposition is through evidence of the defendant's prior bad acts.

North Carolina Rule of Evidence 404(b) governs the admissibility of prior bad acts. It bars evidence of prior crimes, wrongs, or acts by a person to prove the person's character and thereby show that he or she acted in conformity with that character on a particular occasion. For example, the prosecution may not introduce evidence that the defendant sold drugs in the past to show that he or she sold drugs on the present occasion. Rule 404(b) states further, however, that the prosecution may introduce prior conduct for non-character purposes.[2]

One permissible non-character purpose of bad-act evidence specified in Rule 404(b) is "absence of . . . entrapment." Relying on this provision, the North Carolina courts have allowed the prosecution to offer prior bad acts to show the defendant's predisposition to commit the charged offense and thus show the "absence of entrapment."[3] The federal counterpart to Rule 404(b) does not explicitly refer to absence of entrapment as a permissible purpose,[4] but

---

1. *See generally* Sorrells v. United States, 287 U.S. 435, 451–52 (1932) (in its seminal entrapment decision, Court states that defendant who raises entrapment defense may be subjected to "appropriate and searching inquiry" into his or her conduct and predisposition). For a discussion of the predisposition prong, *see supra* § 2.5.

2. The North Carolina courts have generally been liberal in finding permissible, non-character purposes of bad-act evidence. *See generally* State v. Coffey, 326 N.C. 268, 278–79, 389 S.E.2d 48, 54 (1990) (stating that Rule 404(b) is rule of inclusion and that evidence is excluded by rule only if its purpose is to show defendant's propensity to commit charged offense).

3. *See* State v. Goldman, 97 N.C. App. 589, 593, 389 S.E.2d 281, 283–84 (1990) (applying provision). Prior bad acts of the defendant also may be admissible in an entrapment case for non-character purposes other than predisposition. *See, e.g.,* State v. Rosario, 93 N.C. App. 627, 638–39, 379 S.E.2d 434, 440–41 (1989) (evidence of prior sale of cocaine admissible to show intent and conspiracy).

4. *See* State v. DeLeonardo, 315 N.C. 762, 769, 340 S.E.2d 350, 356 (1986) (noting difference in language of federal evidence rule).

decisions interpreting the federal rule likewise allow evidence of prior bad acts to show the defendant's predisposition to commit the current offense.[5] Consequently, in both state and federal cases in which the defendant raises an entrapment defense, what ordinarily would be inadmissible "character" evidence may come in as non-character evidence of "predisposition."[6]

If evidence of prior bad acts is admissible under Rule 404(b), the prosecution may elicit the acts through cross-examination or by extrinsic evidence (that is, the testimony of other witnesses or documentary proof). If the defendant takes the stand—and often he or she will need to do so to sustain an entrapment defense[7]—the prosecution may cross-examine the defendant about the acts. The court of appeals has held that if the evidence of the acts is otherwise admissible, the defendant may not claim the Fifth Amendment privilege against self-incrimination and refuse to answer, even as to acts that are not the subject of the current charges.[8] Of course, in questioning the defendant about prior acts, the prosecution must have a good faith factual basis for believing the defendant committed the acts.[9]

---

5. *See, e.g.,* United States v. Burkley, 591 F.2d 903, 921 (D.C. Cir. 1978) (proof of predisposition is permissible purpose under Federal Evidence Rule 404(b) although not explicitly mentioned in it).

6. *See generally* PAUL MARCUS, THE ENTRAPMENT DEFENSE § 4.17, at 148–52 (2d ed. 1995); Daniel E. Feld, Annotation, *Admissibility of Evidence of Other Offenses in Rebuttal of Defense of Entrapment,* 61 A.L.R.3d 293 (1975). Some courts have found that the defendant's character is directly at issue in entrapment cases; accordingly, rather than rely on Rule 404(b), which allows evidence of prior acts for non-character purposes, they have relied on Rule 405(b), which allows evidence of prior acts to prove character in cases in which character is directly at issue. A majority of courts have not used this alternative rationale in admitting prior acts in entrapment cases. *See* United States v. Richardson, 764 F.2d 1514, 1522 n.2 (11th Cir. 1985) (finding that most courts have analyzed admissibility of predisposition evidence under Rule 404(b)); Fred Warren Bennett, *From* Sorrells *to* Jacobson: *Reflections on Six Decades of Entrapment Law, and Related Defenses, in Federal Court,* 27 WAKE FOREST L. REV. 829, 850–51 & n.167 (1992) (admissibility of predisposition evidence more properly analyzed under Rule 404(b) than Rule 405(b)); *see also infra* § 5.2 notes 44–46 and accompanying text (questioning admissibility of reputation evidence to show defendant's character in entrapment case). Even if followed, this alternative rationale would not appear to broaden the scope of admissible acts, which still would be subject to relevancy and other evidentiary restrictions. *See* 22 CHARLES ALAN WRIGHT & KENNETH W. GRAHAM, JR., FEDERAL PRACTICE AND PROCEDURE § 5235, at 372–79 (1978).

7. The defendant is not necessarily required to take the stand to raise an entrapment defense in North Carolina. *See supra* § 4.3(b) (discussing inconsistent-defense doctrine).

8. *See* State v. Artis, 91 N.C. App. 604, 606–07, 372 S.E.2d 905, 906–07 (1988) (so holding). If the prior acts are used for impeachment purposes, and not for substantive purposes under Rule 404(b), the defendant retains the right to refuse to answer on Fifth Amendment grounds. *See* N.C. R. EVID. 608(b) (so stating); 1 KENNETH S. BROUN, BRANDIS & BROUN ON NORTH CAROLINA EVIDENCE § 133, at 444–45 & n.41 (5th ed. 1998) (discussing rule).

9. *See* United States v. Cunningham, 529 F.2d 884, 887–88 (6th Cir. 1976) (cross-examination about prior acts in entrapment case was based almost entirely on hearsay, suspicion, unverified sources, and unreliable innuendo and was improper; cross-examination may not be used as vehicle for getting improper and inadmissible evidence before jury); *see*

Although the prosecution is often given considerable leeway in offering bad-act evidence in entrapment cases, some limits do exist. The principal ones are relevancy and hearsay, discussed below.[10]

(b) Relevancy Restrictions

Not all prior crimes or wrongs committed by the defendant are admissible under Rule 404(b)—in entrapment cases or in criminal cases generally. The touchstone of admissibility is relevancy to a permissible purpose.[11] For a prior act to be admissible to show the defendant's predisposition in an entrapment case, the prosecution must show that the prior act is relevant to a predisposition to commit the charged offense, not merely to commit criminal acts generally.[12] The probative value of the evidence also must outweigh its potential prejudice to the defendant.[13] The key factors in determining whether prior acts have a sufficient bearing on predisposition are the similarity between the prior and current acts and their proximity in time.[14]

Similarity of Acts. North Carolina has not adopted any set formula for evaluating similarity of prior acts in entrapment cases, comparing

---

generally State v. Flannigan, 78 N.C. App. 629, 338 S.E.2d 109 (1985) (court states generally that prosecution may not cross-examine defendant about other acts without good faith basis for questions; cross-examination cannot be used to inform jury of purported misdeeds of defendant that firsthand knowledge of source does not support).

10. The discussion focuses on the application of Rule 404(b) in entrapment cases. For a more general discussion of the preconditions for admission of 404(b) evidence, *see* 1 BROUN, *supra* note 8, §§ 94–95, at 269–90; ROBERT P. MOSTELLER ET AL., NORTH CAROLINA EVIDENTIARY FOUNDATIONS 197–98 (1998) (describing elements of foundation for 404(b) evidence).

11. *See generally* 1 BROUN, *supra* note 8, § 95, at 275 (touchstone of admissibility under Rule 404(b) is logical relevancy to one of permissible purposes); State v. Willis, 136 N.C. App. 820, 526 S.E.2d 191 (2000) (state failed to show how defendant's prior conviction was relevant to one of permissible purposes under Rule 404(b)).

12. *See* United States v. Blankenship, 775 F.2d 735, 739 (6th Cir. 1985) (admitting all prior criminal acts in entrapment case would be tantamount to allowing proof of bad character generally); *see generally* MOSTELLER ET AL., *supra* note 10, at 196 (noting generally that Rule 404(b) does not permit prosecution to offer other wrongs of defendant simply to prove that he or she is law-breaking person).

13. *See generally* N.C. R. EVID. 403 (providing for exclusion of otherwise relevant evidence because of its potential prejudice); MOSTELLER ET AL., *supra* note 10, at 197 (proponent of 404(b) evidence must show that it is logically relevant to permissible purpose and that its probative value outweighs its prejudicial effect).

14. *See Blankenship*, 775 F.2d at 739 (prior acts in entrapment case must involve "conduct substantially similar and reasonably near in time" to offenses for which defendant is being tried). Similarity and temporal proximity also may be significant in evaluating the use of prior acts for other purposes under Rule 404(b). *See* State v. Artis, 325 N.C. 278, 299, 384 S.E.2d 470, 481 (1989) (stressing these factors in evaluating admissibility of prior sex offenses in sex offense prosecution and finding prior offense sufficiently similar), *vacated on other grounds*, 494 U.S. 1023 (1990); State v. White, 135 N.C. App. 349, 520 S.E.2d 70 (1999) (comparing features of prior and current sex offenses and finding prior offense too dissimilar to be admitted); *see also* 1 BROUN, *supra* note 8, § 94, at 271–73 (prior acts are more likely to be excluded if they are dissimilar in kind or remote in time).

offenses essentially on an ad hoc basis. A helpful approach suggested by a court elsewhere is to compare

- the object of the prior and current crimes (for example, drugs, stolen goods, gambling);
- the methods used in perpetrating the crimes; and
- the mental state involved in commission of the crimes.[15]

The importance of similarity can be seen in North Carolina cases addressing the use of prior offenses to show the defendant's predisposition to commit the charged drug offense. In *State v. Artis,* the court of appeals had no difficulty finding that a sale of cocaine by the defendant was admissible to show his predisposition one month later to engage in the same act (sale) of the same substance (cocaine).[16] In *State v. Salame,* the court of appeals found admissible a prior drug transaction involving a different substance but a similar act. The court found that the defendant's distribution of speed, a form of amphetamine, to another person within weeks of the charged offenses was admissible to rebut the defendant's claim that he had been entrapped into distributing other substances (marijuana and cocaine).[17]

When a prior drug offense involves mere possession, its connection to a later sale is more tenuous and its admissibility not as certain. In *State v. Goldman,* the court of appeals recognized that personal use of drugs is not necessarily synonymous with the intent to sell, distribute, or traffic in drugs, but concluded in the case before it that the defendant's prior use and possession of various drugs (marijuana, cocaine, and LSD) was admissible to show his predisposition to sell some of those substances (cocaine and LSD).[18]

The treatment of non-drug offenses is clearer—courts generally have found them too dissimilar to be admissible on the question of the defendant's predisposition to violate the drug laws.[19] In *Goldman,* the court of appeals

---

15. *See* State v. Gibbons, 519 A.2d 350, 356–57 (N.J. 1987) (breaking down similarity inquiry in entrapment case).

16. 91 N.C. App. 604, 605–07, 372 S.E.2d 905, 906–07 (1988).

17. 24 N.C. App. 1, 9–10, 210 S.E.2d 77, 83–84 (1974) (court also found admissible defendant's statements to undercover officers that he had once smuggled cocaine into country).

18. 97 N.C. App. 589, 595, 389 S.E.2d 281, 284 (1990); *see also Gibbons,* 519 A.2d at 358–59 (reviewing approaches of various jurisdictions and finding that some cases have held that possession of small quantities is consistent with personal use and not sufficiently similar to later distribution of drugs); State v. Stanley, 288 N.C. 19, 32–33, 215 S.E.2d 589, 598 (1975) (defendant entitled to nonsuit; court finds that prior conviction for possession of marijuana did not show predisposition to commit charged offenses of possession of LSD with intent to distribute and distribution of LSD).

19. *See, e.g.,* De Jong v. United States, 381 F.2d 725, 726 (9th Cir. 1967) (proof that a man is a burglar or drunk does not tend to show that he was prepared to deal in narcotics); People v. Placek, 704 N.E.2d 393 (Ill. 1998) (evidence that defendant had dealt in stolen auto parts was inadmissible to show defendant's predisposition to commit drug

did not specifically decide the issue, but it did contrast the case before it, which involved prior drug offenses, with cases involving prior offenses unrelated to drugs, which other courts had found inadmissible.[20]

The discussion of similarity is subject to an important caveat. If the prior act resulted in a criminal conviction, the conviction may be admissible regardless of whether it is similar to the current offense. North Carolina rules liberally allow the use of prior convictions to impeach the credibility of a witness, although when the purpose is to impeach rather than to show predisposition the inquiry is limited to the time and place of conviction and the punishment imposed.[21] Defendants asserting an entrapment defense will ordinarily take the stand to explain their actions,[22] so they will face such impeachment if they have a criminal record.

Timing of Acts. Whether committed before or after the charged offense, similar acts have been found admissible in entrapment cases if not too remote in time. Because acts committed afterward may have less bearing on the defendant's predisposition at the time of the offense, however, the length of time that has elapsed may undergo closer scrutiny.[23] Acts

offense); *Gibbons*, 519 A.2d at 359 (finding that courts generally exclude such evidence); *see also* W. H. Johnson, III, *Proving a Criminal Predisposition: Separating the Unwary Innocent from the Unwary Criminal*, 43 Duke L.J. 384, 394–95 (1993) (noting trend among courts to exclude such evidence); Bennett, *supra* note 6, at 850–51 (to same effect).

20. 97 N.C. App. at 594–95, 389 S.E.2d at 284, *citing* United States v. Daniels, 572 F.2d 535 (5th Cir. 1978) (defendant's possession of sawed-off shotgun was not probative of predisposition to violate drug laws and thus was not admissible). Outside the entrapment context, North Carolina decisions have excluded prior offenses that have no relationship to the current offense. *See, e.g.,* State v. Gordon, 104 N.C. App. 455, 458–59, 410 S.E.2d 4, 7 (1991) (evidence of cocaine use was erroneously admitted in assault case, although error was harmless); State v. Emery, 91 N.C. App. 24, 32–34, 370 S.E.2d 456, 461–62 (1988) (in murder prosecution, evidence of sale of marijuana to victim was properly admitted to show relationship between defendant and victim, but admission of sales to others and unrelated breaking and entering was reversible error).

21. *See* N.C. R. Evid. 609 (for purpose of attacking credibility of witness, evidence of conviction of felony or Class A1, Class 1, or Class 2 misdemeanor within last ten years is admissible); State v. Garner, 330 N.C. 273, 288–89, 410 S.E.2d 861, 869–70 (1991) (inquiry into prior convictions for impeachment purposes is limited to time and place of conviction and punishment imposed).

22. The defendant is not necessarily required to take the stand under North Carolina entrapment law. *See supra* § 4.3(b) (discussing inconsistent-defense doctrine).

23. *Compare* United States v. Jiminez, 613 F.2d 1373, 1376 (5th Cir. 1980) (subsequent offense "certainly bears substantially less on predisposition than would a prior extrinsic offense"; possession of cocaine one year after charge of heroin distribution inadmissible) *with Goldman*, 97 N.C. App. at 594–95, 389 S.E.2d at 284 (distinguishing *Jiminez,* court finds possession of marijuana and cocaine eight days after charged offense admissible). *See also* State v. Dancy, 43 N.C. App. 208, 211–12, 258 S.E.2d 494, 496 (1979) (sale of LSD within one month after charged marijuana sale was admissible); State v. Salame, 24 N.C. App. 1, 9–10, 210 S.E.2d 77, 83–84 (1974) (statements and events within a few weeks after charged offense admissible). In the wake of the U.S. Supreme Court's 1992 decision in *Jacobson*, discussed *supra* § 2.5(c), in which the Court held that predisposition must be measured as of the time of the government's initial contact with the defendant, some federal courts have questioned the relevance of acts committed after the charged offense. *See* United States v. Brooks, 215 F.3d 842, 846 (8th Cir. 2000); United States v. Casanova, 970 F.2d 371, 376 (7th Cir. 1992).

committed by the defendant after the government's initial contact are generally admissible, although they too may have less bearing on the defendant's predisposition before the initial contact, which is the ultimate issue to be resolved in entrapment cases.[24]

(c) Hearsay Restrictions

In addition to being relevant to the defendant's predisposition to commit the charged offense, evidence of prior acts must be in admissible form.[25] An issue that has arisen in entrapment cases is whether hearsay that ordinarily would be inadmissible in other types of cases may be used to show a defendant's predisposition. The trend in the courts is to apply the usual restrictions on hearsay to entrapment cases and to exclude such evidence unless a recognized exception applies.[26] Although no North Carolina case has explicitly addressed the issue, there is little reason to believe that North Carolina would jettison its restrictions on hearsay and follow a different set of rules in entrapment cases.[27]

The application of hearsay restrictions to proof of the defendant's prior acts is illustrated by the Fifth Circuit's opinion in *United States v. Webster.*[28] In *Webster,* in response to the defendant's claim that he had been entrapped into selling cocaine, the prosecution called a Drug Enforcement Administration (DEA) agent to the stand, who testified that an informant said that the defendant had sold cocaine to the in-

---

24. *See* United States v. Rogers, 121 F.3d 12, 17 (1st Cir. 1997) (government permitted to introduce evidence of defendant's behavior after he was approached by government as evidence of predisposition before government contact); *see also supra* § 2.5(c) (predisposition is measured as of time of government's initial contact with defendant).

25. *See generally* 1 Broun, *supra* note 8, § 94, at 273 (prior acts under Rule 404(b) must be "shown by competent evidence").

26. *See, e.g.,* United States v. Hunt, 749 F.2d 1078, 1082 (4th Cir. 1984) (noting that every circuit that has considered question has found that hearsay not within recognized hearsay exception is inadmissible to prove predisposition); United States v. McClain, 531 F.2d 431, 435 (9th Cir. 1976) (use of hearsay to show predisposition impermissible and invokes " 'faceless informer' at his worst"); Lambeth v. State, 562 So. 2d 575, 579 (Ala. 1990) (finding "no justification for the proposition that where the predisposition of the defendant is in issue, traditional hearsay rules are thrown out the window").

27. In one North Carolina case in which the defendant interposed an entrapment defense to a charge of receiving stolen property, a law enforcement officer testified that an informant had told him that the defendant had previously received stolen property. *See* State v. Hageman, 307 N.C. 1, 30–31, 296 S.E.2d 433, 450 (1982). The court did not consider whether this testimony about the informant's out-of-court statements was admissible. Rather, the issue was whether the defendant was entitled to dismissal of the charges in light of all of the evidence presented, including evidence that the state had reasonable suspicion to investigate the defendant based on the information provided by the informant. The court found dismissal unwarranted but also suggested that the state was not required to show the existence of reasonable suspicion to overcome an entrapment defense. This latter observation is consistent with the analysis in *Webster,* discussed *infra* notes 28–32 and accompanying text, which found that reasonable suspicion is ordinarily irrelevant in an entrapment case and therefore out-of-court statements purportedly offered to show reasonable suspicion are usually inadmissible.

28. 649 F.2d 346 (5th Cir. 1981).

formant on several other occasions. The court held that this testimony fell within the classic definition of hearsay—that is, it consisted of an out-of-court statement offered for the truth of the matter asserted in the statement. The court recognized that the prosecution's purpose in offering the informant's statement was to show that the defendant was predisposed to commit the offense of selling cocaine. The court recognized further that the statement was relevant in showing the defendant's predisposition only if it were true. Finding no applicable exception, the court ruled the out-of-court statement inadmissible.[29]

The *Webster* court rejected the government's argument that the informant's statements were offered for a purpose other than their truth—that is, to show that the DEA had reasonable grounds for investigating the defendant. The court found that the good or bad faith of law enforcement officers is generally not at issue in an entrapment case; rather, the focus of the entrapment defense is on the defendant's state of mind. Consequently, even if offered for that purpose, the informant's statements would still be excludable as irrelevant.[30]

The court also indicated that in some instances a defendant may open the door to evidence of the government's reasons for its investigation, including evidence in the form of out-of-court statements to government agents. Such evidence may become relevant if the defendant offers evidence that the government acted in bad faith—for example, evidence that a particular agent was out to get the defendant because of some personal animosity.[31] A defendant also may be found to have opened the door to out-of-court statements by attacking as outrageous the government's decision to launch an investigation against him or her. In *United States v. Hunt,* the Fourth Circuit held that the defendant's presentation of such a claim as part of a Due Process defense opened the door to rebuttal evidence that the government had reasonable grounds for initiating its investigation.[32]

---

29. *Id.* at 349–51; *see also* United States v. Nixon, 777 F.2d 958, 964 (5th Cir. 1985) (reaffirming *Webster* but finding that out-of-court statements by defendant about prior bad acts were admissible under exception for admissions of party-opponent).

30. *Webster,* 649 F.2d at 349–51 (also noting that any probative value is outweighed by prejudicial effect because jury might consider out-of-court statements as evidence of predisposition or bad character); *see also McClain,* 531 F.2d at 435–37 (it is not state of mind of government agent that is important; it is defendant's predisposition—that is, his or her state of mind—that counts).

31. *Webster,* 649 F.2d at 351.

32. 749 F.2d 1078, 1083–84 (4th Cir. 1984). The Fourth Circuit noted that since the trial judge, not the jury, is responsible for deciding a Due Process defense of outrageous conduct (*see supra* § 3.3(b)), various procedural devices may be available to keep otherwise inadmissible evidence from the jury or minimize its impact. 749 F.2d at 1084 n.8 (noting that defendant could seek limiting instruction or enter into stipulation with government). The dissent in *Webster,* at 649 F.2d at 352–53, argued that a defendant who asserts an entrapment defense always opens the door to evidence about the government's reasons for its investigation because such a defense necessarily impugns the government's motives. The majority in *Webster* and the Fourth Circuit in *Hunt* rejected this approach, recognizing that merely raising the entrapment defense does not open the door to otherwise inadmissible hearsay.

Under North Carolina law, an officer also might be permitted to testify to statements an informant made about the defendant's prior activities if the informant takes the stand and testifies to those activities. In those circumstances, the officer's testimony may be admissible for the limited purpose of corroborating the informant's testimony.[33]

(d) Prior Good Acts

Just as the prosecution may not offer prior bad acts for the purpose of showing that the defendant committed the current offense, the defendant may not offer prior good acts (or lack of bad acts) to show that he or she did not commit the current offense. When offered for this purpose, good acts violate Rule 404(b)'s prohibition on the use of character to prove conduct.[34]

Because Rule 404(b) allows evidence of prior acts for non-character purposes, however, it may allow a defendant who claims entrapment to present evidence of his or her prior good conduct (or lack of bad conduct) to show lack of predisposition. The Ninth Circuit reached this result in *United States v. Thomas,* holding that evidence of the defendant's prior good conduct, including lack of any criminal record, was admissible to show lack of predisposition.[35]

The North Carolina courts have not specifically ruled on this question, although in *State v. Hageman* the court suggested that prior good acts might negate predisposition.[36] In other cases, the North Carolina courts have implicitly recognized the potential relevance of prior good conduct on the question of predisposition, relying on such evidence in evaluating the appropriateness of giving jury instructions on entrapment or dismissing the charges altogether.[37]

---

33. *See* State v. Broome, 136 N.C. App. 82, 91, 523 S.E.2d 448, 455 (1999); *see also* 1 BROUN, *supra* note 8, § 165, at 528–34 (discussing application of North Carolina rule and criticisms of it); N.C. R. EVID. 403 (evidence may be excluded if probative value is outweighed by danger of unfair prejudice, confusion of issues, or misleading jury). If the testimony is admitted for this purpose, the defendant would be entitled on request to a limiting instruction to the jury.

34. *See generally* State v. Bogle, 324 N.C. 190, 200, 376 S.E.2d 745, 750–51 (1989) (court holds generally that defendant may not offer lack of criminal record to show good character); 1 BROUN, *supra* note 8, § 97, at 297. Notwithstanding this general ban on the use of specific acts, the accused in a criminal case may always offer opinion and reputation evidence of a pertinent character trait (such as being law-abiding) to show that he or she acted in conformity with that trait. *See infra* § 5.2 notes 42–45 and accompanying text.

35. 134 F.3d 975 (9th Cir. 1998); *accord* Sykes v. State, 739 So. 2d 641 (Fla. Dist. Ct. App. 1999).

36. 307 N.C. 1, 25, 296 S.E.2d 433, 447 (1982) (in reviewing trial court's denial of jury instructions requested by defendant, court reaffirmed general rule that good character may not be shown by specific acts but left open possibility that defendant might be entitled to jury instruction that lack of predisposition may be shown by specific acts).

37. *See* State v. Stanley, 288 N.C. 19, 24, 215 S.E.2d 589, 593 (1975) (in finding that defendant was entitled to nonsuit, court notes that defendant had never used drugs of type solicited by undercover officer); *see also* State v. Jamerson, 64 N.C. App. 301,

§ 5.2   Reputation Evidence

Courts have stated in entrapment cases that the defendant's character or reputation is relevant to the question of whether he or she was predisposed to commit the charged offense.[38] This proposition is unobjectionable if the terms "character" and "reputation" are taken in a general, nontechnical sense. Relevant past behavior, if shown by competent evidence, is unquestionably admissible under Rule 404(b) on the question of predisposition.[39] If the terms are taken in their technical, evidentiary sense, however, the proposition is problematic. The use of true character evidence, of which reputation testimony is one form, is strictly controlled. In the only reported North Carolina case that has addressed the issue, the court stated generally that "competent reputation testimony can be used to establish predisposition," but it did not address how limited the scope of "competent" reputation evidence is and did not actually rule on the admissibility of the contested evidence.[40]

Three intersecting rules affect the use of character and reputation evidence.[41] North Carolina Evidence Rule 404(a)(1) allows the accused in a criminal case to offer evidence of a pertinent trait of his or her character to show that he or she acted in conformity with that character trait on a particular occasion. If the defendant introduces evidence of his or her character, the prosecution may offer character evidence about the defendant in rebuttal. This rule creates a narrow exception to the general prohibition on the use of character to prove conduct.[42]

302, 307 S.E.2d 436, 436–37 (1983) (court relies on defendant's initial refusals to engage in criminal activity in finding that trial court erred in refusing to instruct on entrapment); Kent v. State, 704 So. 2d 121, 125 (Fla. Dist. Ct. App. 1997) (holding that defendant's initial refusals to sell cocaine to undercover officers were relevant to lack of predisposition).

38. *See, e.g.,* United States v. Navarro, 737 F.2d 625, 635 (7th Cir. 1984) (listing character or reputation as one of factors in determining predisposition).

39. *See supra* § 5.1.

40. State v. Goldman, 97 N.C. App. 589, 595–96, 389 S.E.2d 281, 284–85 (1990). The court did not decide the issue because the trial judge, after initially allowing certain hearsay evidence purportedly showing the defendant's predisposition, ruled it inadmissible and instructed the jury to disregard it. In the course of its discussion, the *Goldman* court cited a Fifth Circuit decision stating that the government could use hearsay evidence, even if not within any exception, to show predisposition. That line of decisions has been overruled. *See* United States v. Webster, 649 F.2d 346 (5th Cir. 1981), discussed *supra* notes 28–32 and accompanying text.

41. The rules discussed here deal with the use of character evidence for substantive purposes. Other rules, not at issue here, deal with its use to impeach a witness's credibility. *See* N.C. R. Evid. 608 (evidence of character for truthfulness), 609 (impeachment by conviction of crime).

42. *See generally* State v. Sexton, 336 N.C. 321, 359–60, 444 S.E.2d 879, 901 (1994) (stating that this exception should be restrictively construed).

Evidence Rule 405 describes the permissible methods of proving character, stating that in cases in which evidence of character is admissible, proof may be made in the form of reputation or opinion testimony. Rule 405 also provides that specific acts of the defendant are admissible to establish character in some circumstances—namely, on cross-examination of a reputation or opinion witness and in cases in which character is directly at issue. The extent to which Rule 405 allows evidence of specific acts to show character is not as critical in entrapment cases because Rule 404(b) permits the use of prior acts for the non-character purpose of showing predisposition. The focus of this discussion is the extent to which reputation (and opinion) testimony is admissible to show character.

The last pertinent rule on character evidence, Rule 803(21), provides that reputation of a person's character among his or her associates or in the community is excepted from the rules barring hearsay. This exception is necessary because reputation testimony about character is a form of hearsay. When a witness testifies about a person's reputation, he or she essentially is reporting in shorthand form what others in the community have said about the person—in other words, out-of-court statements. When offered to show that a person acted in conformity with his or her character—and that is ordinarily the purpose of such testimony—the testimony is offered for the truth of the matter asserted and thus must satisfy this hearsay exception as well as the above rules on the use of character evidence.[43]

These rules create three hurdles for a prosecutor seeking to offer reputation testimony about a defendant in an entrapment case. The first hurdle, erected by Rule 404(a)(1), is that the defendant must place his or her character in issue before the prosecution may offer reputation (or opinion) testimony in rebuttal. Some courts have held that the defendant does not place his or her character in issue simply by raising an entrapment defense.[44]

A second problem is that reputation testimony is admissible only on a pertinent "trait of character." For example, the defendant may offer reputation or opinion evidence that he or she is law-abiding, and the prosecution then may rebut the same. Being law-abiding is a recognized character trait, pertinent in virtually all criminal cases because

---

43. *See generally* 1 Broun, *supra* note 8, § 86, at 254–56 (ordinarily reputation is offered as evidence of character and for this purpose is species of hearsay); N.C. R. Evid. 803(21) commentary (discussing relationship between this hearsay exception and rules on character evidence); *see also* State v. Crawford, 104 N.C. App. 591, 597–98, 410 S.E.2d 499, 502–03 (1991) (recognizing that reputation of defendant's neighborhood is form of hearsay).

44. *See* United States v. Richardson, 764 F.2d 1514, 1522 n.2 (11th Cir. 1985) (so finding); *see also supra* § 5.1(a) note 6 (majority of courts admit prior bad acts in entrapment cases because Rule 404(b) allows such evidence for non character purpose of showing predisposition, not because defendant's character is directly at issue).

the defendant is accused of violating the law.[45] Predisposition may not constitute a character trait, however. Some courts have held that it is "a state of mind, not a character trait" and therefore have disallowed testimony about the defendant having a reputation for engaging in conduct similar to the charged crime.[46]

A third restriction on reputation testimony concerns the source and substance of such testimony. Only a witness with personal knowledge of a person's reputation in the community may testify as to that reputation and then may do so only in general terms. Thus, even if an informant who is familiar with the defendant's reputation in the community could testify as to the defendant's reputation, an officer may not testify as to what the informant said to him or her about the defendant's reputation. Although reputation testimony is excepted from the hearsay rule, such double hearsay is not. Similarly, an officer may not testify as to an informant's statements to him or her regarding specific acts by the defendant to show the defendant's reputation. Apart from constituting hearsay, testimony about specific acts is not proper reputation testimony.[47]

These rules restrict the use of reputation (and opinion) testimony only. They do not affect the ability of the prosecution to offer, through

---

45. *See, e.g.,* State v. Bogle, 324 N.C. 190, 199–200, 376 S.E.2d 745, 750 (1989) (on request, defendant is entitled to instruction to jury that it may consider reputation testimony about defendant's character for being law-abiding as substantive evidence of his innocence). Other examples of pertinent character traits are peacefulness in a case in which the defendant is charged with a crime of violence, and honesty in a case in which the defendant is charged with embezzlement. *See* N.C. R. EVID. 404 commentary.

46. United States v. Webster, 649 F.2d 346, 350 (5th Cir. 1981); *accord Richardson,* 764 F.2d at 1522 n.2. *See also* State v. Hageman, 307 N.C. 1, 25, 296 S.E.2d 433, 447 (1982) (suggesting that character and predisposition are distinct); *but see* Johnson, *supra* note 19, at 406–07 (author argues that, under comparable federal evidence rules, government may present evidence that defendant had reputation for engaging in type of illegal activity with which he or she is charged; author fails to address whether such behavior constitutes a character trait). In some cases not involving entrapment, the state has sought to offer reputation testimony that the defendant was a drug dealer, and the court has disallowed the testimony because the defendant had not yet placed his or her character in issue. *See, e.g.,* State v. Taylor, 117 N.C. App. 644, 651–52, 453 S.E.2d 225, 229–30 (1995). Perhaps a bigger problem with such testimony is that while one may have a reputation for being a drug dealer, it is questionable whether engaging in such behavior is a trait of character, provable by reputation testimony. *See generally* State v. Collins, 345 N.C. 170, 173–74, 478 S.E.2d 191, 193–94 (1996) (evidence focused on factual information about defendant's behavior, not character trait); *Bogle,* 324 N.C. at 200, 376 S.E.2d at 750–51 (evidence of lack of criminal record is a "fact," not a character trait). Nor would it appear proper to introduce a person's reputation for being a drug dealer as a way of showing the person's bad character in general. *Compare* State v. Squire, 321 N.C. 541, 546–47, 364 S.E.2d 354, 357–58 (1988) (to be admissible under North Carolina Rules of Evidence, character evidence must concern particular trait of person's character, not general character) *with* State v. Turner, 66 N.C. App. 203, 210–11, 311 S.E.2d 331, 336 (1984) (in case decided before adoption of evidence rules, court allowed evidence of defendant's bad character, as shown by reputation for drug dealing, to rebut evidence of defendant's general good character).

47. *See Webster,* 649 F.2d at 349–50 & n.7; Johnson, *supra* note 19, at 407–08 (recognizing that even if reputation testimony about the defendant's predisposition is admissible, hearsay evidence of the defendant's reputation is not).

non-hearsay evidence, relevant instances of conduct by the defendant. Such evidence is admissible under Rule 404(b) for the non-character purpose of showing predisposition and is not subject to the highly structured rules on proving character.

§ 5.3   CONVERSATIONS WITH OFFICERS AND INFORMANTS

Statements made by undercover officers and informants are often critical to a defendant's presentation of an entrapment defense. Such statements are relevant because they bear directly on whether the defendant acted in response to some inducement by an agent of the government. They also fall outside the ban on hearsay because, although out-of-court statements, they ordinarily are not offered for the truth of the matter asserted. For example, in one North Carolina case the defendant sought to testify that a government informant repeatedly asked the defendant to get him some heroin because the informant said that he was sick and needed it. The court held that the statements were not offered for the truth of the matter asserted—that is, that the informant was actually sick—but instead were offered to show "that the statements were made, and that through them, defendant was induced to commit an offense he would not otherwise have committed."[48] Even if offered for their truth, statements by agents of the government may be admissible under the exception for admissions of a party-opponent.[49]

If offered by the defendant, his or her own statements to undercover officers or informants do not come within the hearsay exception for admissions of a party-opponent. But a defendant who relies on an entrapment defense will often be able to introduce his or her statements under the hearsay exception for statements of then-existing state of mind.[50]

§ 5.4   EXPERT TESTIMONY

North Carolina Rule of Evidence 702 permits expert testimony if it will assist the trier of fact in understanding the evidence or determining a fact in issue. Federal courts have found under a comparable evidence rule that a defendant relying on an entrapment defense may offer expert

---

48. State v. Brockenborough, 45 N.C. App. 121, 122, 262 S.E.2d 330, 331 (1980); *see also* State v. Worthington, 84 N.C. App. 150, 156, 352 S.E.2d 695, 699–700 (1987) (trial court erred in excluding defendant's testimony about informant's statements, but error was not prejudicial because excluded evidence was otherwise presented to jury).

49. *See* N.C. R. EVID. 801(d) (exception for admission of party-opponent); *see also* United States v. Branham, 97 F.3d 835, 850–51 (6th Cir. 1996) (statements of government informant constituted admissions of party-opponent).

50. *See* N.C. R. EVID. 803(3); *see also* Kent v. State, 704 So. 2d 121, 125 (Fla. Dist. Ct. App. 1997) (holding that evidence of defendant's initial refusals to sell cocaine to undercover officers did not constitute hearsay because they were offered to show lack of

testimony on his or her unusual susceptibility to inducement.[51] The North Carolina courts have not addressed the issue in entrapment cases, although they have allowed expert testimony about the defendant's mental condition in cases involving the defense of duress and other forms of compulsion.[52] Because expert testimony about susceptibility to inducement concerns the defendant's mental state, it would not appear to run afoul of North Carolina Evidence Rule 405(a), which proscribes expert testimony on character as circumstantial evidence of behavior.[53] Whether the defendant would have to give notice of an intent to rely on such expert testimony in an entrapment case is unclear.[54]

---

predisposition); *Branham*, 97 F.3d at 851 (conversation between informant and defendant was not offered for truth but rather to show defendant's state of mind); *cf.* State v. Moore, 41 N.C. App. 148, 151–52, 254 S.E.2d 252, 254 (1979) (defendant's statement to sister after his arrest that he had been "trapped" was properly excluded as irrelevant).

51. *See* United States v. Newman, 849 F.2d 156, 163–66 (5th Cir. 1988) (in reliance on authority from several other circuits, court holds that such testimony is admissible but concludes that trial court did not abuse discretion in finding that particular testimony offered by defendant would confuse jury); *accord* United States v. Nunn, 940 F.2d 1148, 1149 (8th Cir. 1991).

52. *See* State v. Gay, 334 N.C. 467, 484–85, 434 S.E.2d 840, 849–50 (1993) (expert testimony in support of duress defense); State v. Baldwin, 125 N.C. App. 530, 535–36, 482 S.E.2d 1, 5 (1997) (expert testimony in support of claim of false confession under police interrogation).

53. *See generally Baldwin*, 125 N.C. App. at 535–36, 482 S.E.2d at 5 (expert testimony about defendant's mental condition was not prohibited character evidence; trial court erred in excluding expert testimony about psychological factors that would make defendant more prone to make false confession); *see also supra* § 5.2 notes 45–46 and accompanying text (predisposition is state of mind, not character trait).

54. *Compare* N.C. GEN. STAT. 15A-959(b) (defendant must give timely notice of intent to introduce expert testimony relating to mental disease, defect, or other condition bearing on whether he or she had mental state required for offense charged) *with* State v. Hageman, 307 N.C. 1, 26–27, 296 S.E.2d 433, 448 (1982) (in discussing whether defendant may be required to bear burden of proving entrapment, court states that predisposition is not element of offense).

6   Burdens and Instructions

§ 6.1   BURDEN OF PLEADING   77

§ 6.2   BURDENS OF PROOF   77

     (a)   Persuading the Jury   78

     (b)   Obtaining Jury Instructions   79

     (c)   Avoiding or Obtaining Nonsuit   82

§ 6.3   JURY INSTRUCTIONS   83

     (a)   Giving of Instructions   83

     (b)   Wording of Instructions   84

6   Burdens and Instructions

A basic tenet of criminal law is that the prosecution bears the burden of proving the defendant's guilt beyond a reasonable doubt. Although this principle applies in cases involving claims of entrapment, more complex burdens come into play. This chapter considers how those burdens operate in entrapment cases as well as instructions to be given to the jury in cases in which the defendant has presented sufficient evidence of entrapment to warrant instructions.[1]

§ 6.1   BURDEN OF PLEADING

Although not typically thought of as a burden, parties in criminal cases may have a *burden of pleading*, or alleging, their claims and defenses. Thus the prosecution has the burden of properly alleging in the indictment or other pleading the offenses with which the defendant is charged. The only burden of pleading imposed on the defendant under North Carolina law appears in Section 15A-959(a) of the North Carolina General Statutes, which requires the defendant to give notice of intent to raise an insanity defense. There is no comparable requirement pertaining to entrapment or other defenses.[2]

§ 6.2   BURDENS OF PROOF

The term *burden of proof* actually refers to two separate burdens—the burden of production and the burden of persuasion. The party with the *burden of production* on a particular issue must present sufficient

---

1. The discussion here concerns the entrapment defense only and not related defenses, such as want-of-element defenses. For a discussion of burdens applicable to those defenses, refer to the applicable section in Chapter 3, "Related Defenses."

2. *See generally* State v. Ross, 329 N.C. 108, 112–14, 405 S.E.2d 158, 161 (1991) (court disapproves of trial court order requiring defendant to give notice of intent to rely on self-defense). It is not clear whether a defendant who intends to rely on expert testimony about his or her susceptibility to inducement in support of an entrapment defense must give notice of that intent under N.C. GEN. STAT. 15A-959(b). *See supra* § 5.4 note 54 and accompanying text.

evidence to warrant submitting the issue to the jury for decision. The party with the *burden of persuasion* on a particular issue must present sufficient evidence to justify a finding by the jury in the party's favor.[3]

(a) Persuading the Jury

In entrapment cases as in all criminal cases, the prosecution bears the burden of persuading the jury of the defendant's guilt. To meet this burden, the prosecution must prove all of the essential elements of the charged offense beyond a reasonable doubt.[4]

On the question of entrapment, however, North Carolina places the burden of persuasion on the defendant to prove both prongs of the defense—inducement by the government and lack of predisposition by the defendant. The applicable standard is proof to the jury's satisfaction,[5] a standard no greater than proof by a preponderance of the evidence.[6]

Defendants have argued that at least on the question of predisposition, which is intertwined with criminal intent, the burden of persuasion should be on the state. The North Carolina courts have rejected that argument, however, holding that predisposition is separate from the mental state required for conviction and that the defendant may be constitutionally required to bear the burden of proving lack of predisposition.[7]

In allocating to the defendant the burden of persuasion on both prongs of the entrapment defense, North Carolina differs from most jurisdictions that use the subjective test of entrapment. Although jurisdictions vary on whether and to what extent the defendant must prove government inducement,[8] most agree that the prosecution bears the

---

3. *See generally* 1 KENNETH S. BROUN, BRANDIS & BROUN ON NORTH CAROLINA EVIDENCE §§ 32–33, at 115–20 (5th ed. 1998); 1 WAYNE R. LaFAVE & AUSTIN W. SCOTT, JR. SUBSTANTIVE CRIMINAL LAW § 1.8(a), at 67 (1986).

4. *See* Apprendi v. New Jersey, 530 U.S. 466 (2000); Mullaney v. Wilbur, 421 U.S. 684 (1975); *In re* Winship, 397 U.S. 358 (1970).

5. *See* State v. Cook, 263 N.C. 730, 733, 140 S.E.2d 305, 308 (1965); State v. Parker, 61 N.C. App. 585, 587, 301 S.E.2d 450, 451 (1983).

6. *See generally* 1 BROUN, *supra* note 3, § 43, at 142–43; State v. Payne, 337 N.C. 505, 532, 448 S.E.2d 93, 109 (1994) (in assessing standard for proving mitigating circumstance in capital case, court states that proof to jury's satisfaction "denotes a burden of proof consistent with a preponderance of the evidence"); State v. Hankerson, 288 N.C. 632, 648, 220 S.E.2d 575, 587 (1975) (in assessing standard for rebutting presumption of malice in homicide case, court states that proof to jury's satisfaction is "a standard not greater and at the same time one not significantly less than persuasion by a preponderance of the evidence"), *rev'd on other grounds*, 432 U.S. 233 (1977).

7. *See* State v. Hageman, 307 N.C. 1, 26–28, 296 S.E.2d 433, 448–49 (1982).

8. Some jurisdictions hold that although the defendant must meet an initial burden of producing evidence in support of an entrapment defense, the prosecution has the ultimate burden of proving beyond a reasonable doubt that the defendant was not entrapped; in those jurisdictions, the defendant bears no burden of persuasion on either prong of the defense. Others require the defendant to shoulder the ultimate burden of proving inducement, by a preponderance of the evidence or equivalent standard. *See* authorities cited *infra* note 9.

burden of proving beyond a reasonable doubt that the defendant was predisposed to commit the charged offense.[9]

(b) Obtaining Jury Instructions

Generally. Before the court is required to submit the issue of entrapment to the jury, the defendant must meet an initial burden of production. This burden acts as a screening device. It serves to prevent the defendant from obtaining instructions on defenses supported by mere conjecture or speculation but is not intended to be so rigorous as to keep the jury from receiving instructions on and deciding defenses for which supporting evidence exists.[10]

The North Carolina courts have used different formulations to describe the defendant's burden of production for different defenses. For example, for self-defense the standard is "any" evidence in support of the elements of self-defense; for diminished capacity, the standard is sufficient evidence "reasonably to warrant inference of the fact at issue."[11] The difference in phrasing apparently reflects a judgment by the North Carolina courts about the relative merits of different defenses— the less rigorous the standard, the more favored the defense.[12] As a practical matter, however, it is unclear whether the difference has much effect on whether the defendant is able to obtain instructions.[13]

---

9. *See generally* 2 WAYNE R. LaFAVE ET AL., CRIMINAL PROCEDURE § 5.3(d), at 423–24 (2d ed. 1999); PAUL MARCUS, THE ENTRAPMENT DEFENSE § 6.05, at 211, § 6.07, at 217–18 (2d ed. 1995); John H. Derrick, Annotation, *Burden of Proof as to Entrapment Defense—State Cases*, 52 A.L.R.4th 775 (1987); Annotation, *Instructing on Burden of Proof as to Defense of Entrapment in Federal Criminal Case*, 28 A.L.R. FED. 767 (1976).

10. *See generally* 1 PAUL H. ROBINSON, CRIMINAL LAW DEFENSES § 4(a), at 20–26, § 33(b), at 130–36 (1984). Some have argued that placing a burden of production on the defendant on any issue relating to culpability relieves the state of its burden of persuasion on all essential facts and invades the province of the jury. *See* Ronald J. Allen, *Structuring Jury Decisionmaking in Criminal Cases: A Unified Constitutional Approach to Evidentiary Devices*, 94 HARV. L. REV. 321, 327–29, 358–60 (1980). It is generally accepted, however, that some burden of production for defenses may be placed on the defendant. *Cf.* Montana v. Egelhoff, 518 U.S. 37 (1996) (finding no constitutional violation in Montana statute that provided that voluntary intoxication could not even be considered by jury in determining existence of mental state required for conviction of offense).

11. *See* State v. Clark, 324 N.C. 146, 161–63, 377 S.E.2d 54, 63–64 (1989) (contrasting burdens of production for self-defense and diminished capacity; also noting that burden of production to obtain instruction on lesser offense is "any" evidence); *see also* John Rubin, THE LAW OF SELF-DEFENSE IN NORTH CAROLINA § 8.2(c), at 186–87 & n.11 (Institute of Government, 1996); John Rubin, *The Diminished Capacity Defense*, ADMINISTRATION OF JUSTICE MEMORANDUM No. 92/01, at 6 (Institute of Government, 1992).

12. *See Clark,* 324 N.C. at 162, 377 S.E.2d at 64 (test is less rigorous when defendant offers evidence in support of defense based on circumstances beyond his or her control, such as self-defense).

13. *See generally* State v. Fields, 324 N.C. 204, 209–10, 376 S.E.2d 740, 743 (1989) (where defendant's evidence discloses facts that are legally sufficient to constitute defense to crime charged, court is required to instruct jury on legal principles applicable to defense). The main exception is voluntary intoxication, a defense for which the North Carolina courts have set a relatively high burden of production. *See Clark,* 324 N.C. at 161–62, 377 S.E.2d at 63–64; *see also* John Rubin, *The Voluntary Intoxication Defense*, ADMINISTRATION OF JUSTICE MEMORANDUM No. 93/01, at 10–11 (Institute of Government, 1993).

Standard for Entrapment. The North Carolina courts have held in entrapment cases that the defendant meets the initial burden of production by producing "some credible evidence" on both prongs of the defense— inducement and lack of predisposition.[14] In several cases the appellate courts have found that the defendant met this burden and so was entitled to instructions on entrapment.[15] There are, of course, numerous cases going the other way.[16] It is difficult to generalize from these cases exactly what evidence the defendant must produce to be assured of obtaining instructions on entrapment. Each case depends on the evidence presented and whether it falls within the general contours of entrapment drawn by the North Carolina courts.[17] Some general observations are possible, however, about the amount and nature of proof required of the defendant under the "some credible evidence" standard.

Threshold of Proof. How much evidence must the defendant produce to obtain instructions on entrapment? Consistent with the general purpose of burdens of production for criminal law defenses, the threshold of proof appears to be relatively low: merely "some" evidence. Although it is difficult to state precisely how much evidence is "some" under this standard, it presumably is well less than the amount necessary to meet the defendant's burden of persuasion—proof to the jury's satisfaction.[18] Although the courts have also stated that the evidence must be "credible," it seems unlikely that they intended for trial judges to make credibility determinations in deciding the defendant's entitlement to instructions. Trial judges must determine initially whether the evidence meets the legal requirements of entrapment (and other defenses), but the question of whether to believe or disbelieve the evidence is generally for the jury to resolve.[19] Apparently no reported decisions

14. *See* State v. Walker, 295 N.C. 510, 513, 246 S.E.2d 748, 749 (1978) (so holding); *accord* State v. Luster, 306 N.C. 566, 571, 295. S.E.2d 421, 424 (1982); State v. Burnette, 242 N.C. 164, 173, 87 S.E.2d 191, 197 (1955).

15. *See, e.g.,* State v. Sanders, 95 N.C. App. 56, 381 S.E.2d 827 (1989) (evidence warranted instructions); State v. Blackwell, 67 N.C. App. 432, 313 S.E.2d 797 (1984); State v. Walker, 66 N.C. App. 367, 311 S.E.2d 329 (1984); State v. Jamerson, 64 N.C. App. 301, 303–04, 307 S.E.2d 436, 437–38 (1983); State v. Whisnant, 36 N.C. App. 252, 243 S.E.2d 395 (1978); State v. Bradshaw, 12 N.C. App. 510, 514, 183 S.E.2d 787, 789–90 (1971).

16. *See, e.g., Walker,* 295 N.C. 510, 246 S.E.2d 748 (request for instructions properly denied; Exum, J., dissenting); State v. Jackson, 243 N.C. 216, 90 S.E.2d 507 (1955); State v. Bailey, 93 N.C. App. 721, 723–24, 379 S.E.2d 266, 267–68 (1989); State v. Rosario, 93 N.C. App. 627, 635–37, 379 S.E.2d 434, 438–39 (1989); State v. Martin, 77 N.C. App. 61, 65–67, 334 S.E.2d 459, 461–63 (1985); State v. Thomas, 52 N.C. App. 186, 202–03, 278 S.E.2d 535, 546 (1981); State v. Stanback, 19 N.C. App. 375, 376–77, 198 S.E.2d 759, 760 (1973).

17. For a detailed discussion of the elements of entrapment, *see supra* Chapter 2, "Rules of Entrapment."

18. *See supra* § 6.2(a).

19. *See generally* State v. Bryant, 334 N.C. 333, 337–38, 432 S.E.2d 291, 294 (1993) (under standard for determining whether state has produced sufficient evidence to warrant submitting offense to jury, credibility of witnesses and weight to give testimony is

have actually denied entrapment instructions on the ground that the defendant's evidence was not credible.

A possible interpretation of the "some credible evidence" requirement is that it is equivalent to the "substantial evidence" standard used by the North Carolina courts in evaluating whether the state has offered sufficient evidence in support of an offense to warrant submitting it to the jury. That standard, which requires "such relevant evidence as a reasonable mind might accept as adequate to support a conclusion,"[20] would appear consistent with the goal of screening out issues for which there is no supporting evidence.

Regardless of how the burden of production for entrapment is interpreted, the defendant is aided in meeting it by the general principle that the court must construe the evidence in the light most favorable to the defendant, giving the defendant the benefit of every reasonable inference.[21] The court also must consider any evidence favorable to the defendant, whether presented by the defendant or by the state.[22] These principles allow for the possibility that the jury may credit all of the evidence that supports the defendant's entrapment claim.

Elements of Proof. On what aspects of entrapment must the defendant produce evidence? As indicated, the North Carolina courts have stated that the defendant must offer evidence on both prongs of the defense, inducement and lack of predisposition. The courts also have stated generally that, under the subjective test of entrapment, the defendant's predisposition is critical.[23] Yet in ruling on instruction requests, the North Carolina courts have focused more on the government's actions than on the defendant's mental state.

Generally, in cases in which the North Carolina courts have denied instructions, the reason given has been insufficient evidence of inducement or insufficient evidence of inducement and lack of predisposition.

for jury to decide; only when evidence is inherently incredible may court disregard it), *vacated on other grounds,* 511 U.S. 1001 (1994); State v. Fields, 324 N.C. 204, 209–10, 376 S.E.2d 740, 743 (1989) (if evidence discloses facts that are legally sufficient to constitute defense, weight, if any, to give to evidence is for jury to determine); United States v. Becerra, 992 F.2d 960, 964 (9th Cir. 1993) (weight and credibility of conflicting testimony are issues for jury; trial judge erred in failing to instruct on entrapment).

20. State v. Smith, 300 N.C. 71, 78–79, 265 S.E.2d 164, 169 (1980).

21. *See, e.g.,* State v. Mash, 323 N.C. 339, 348, 372 S.E.2d 532, 537–38 (1988) ("When determining whether the evidence is sufficient to entitle a defendant to jury instructions on a defense or mitigating factor, courts must consider the evidence in the light most favorable to defendant"); *Smith,* 300 N.C. at 78, 265 S.E.2d at 169 (using this standard for evaluating whether state is entitled to have offense charged submitted to jury); State v. Walker, 66 N.C. App. 367, 368, 311 S.E.2d 329, 330 (1984) (applying this principle to entrapment claim).

22. *See, e.g., Mash,* 323 N.C. at 346, 372 S.E.2d at 536 (stating this principle); State v. Braun, 31 N.C. App. 101, 102–03, 228 S.E.2d 466, 467 (1976) (finding that defendant, who presented no evidence, was entitled to jury instruction on entrapment based on state's evidence alone).

23. *See supra* § 2.5(a) (discussing predisposition prong).

Far rarer are decisions upholding the denial of instructions solely for insufficient evidence of lack of predisposition.[24] This result is explainable in part by the factual nature of the predisposition inquiry. Predisposition, like other mental states, often involves factual issues, which ordinarily are for the jury, not for the court, to resolve.[25] In addition, when the evidence is sufficient to show some inducement by the government, that evidence also tends to support the defendant's claim that he or she would not have committed the offense in the absence of the inducement.[26]

(c) Avoiding or Obtaining Nonsuit

Just as the prosecution has the burden of proving to the jury the elements of the offense, it also has the burden of producing sufficient evidence to justify submitting the charged offense to the jury. For the prosecution to meet this initial burden of production, the trial court must find that a rational trier of fact could accept the evidence as proof of the defendant's guilt beyond a reasonable doubt.[27] The prosecution is aided in meeting this burden by the principle that the court must consider the evidence in the light most favorable to the prosecution, giving the prosecution the benefit of every reasonable inference.[28] If the prosecution fails to meet its burden of production, the court must grant the defendant's motion for dismissal or nonsuit. These principles apply regardless of whether the defendant relies on entrapment as a defense.

In cases involving entrapment claims, the prosecution also may suffer nonsuit if the evidence establishes entrapment as a matter of law. Dismissal of the charges is required if the undisputed evidence would compel

---

24. *See, e.g.*, State v. Luster, 306 N.C. 566, 574–582, 295 S.E.2d 421, 426–430 (1982) (court based denial of instructions primarily on finding that evidence showed that defendants were predisposed to commit charged crimes, but court also relied on absence of government inducement; dissent found sufficient evidence to support entrapment instructions).

25. *See generally* MARCUS, *supra* note 9, § 4.10, at 130.

26. *See supra* § 2.5(b) note 66 and accompanying text (strength of inducement is one of factors in determining predisposition).

27. *See* Jackson v. Virginia, 443 U.S. 307, 318–19 (1979) (using standard stated in text); State v. Jones, 303 N.C. 500, 503–05, 279 S.E.2d 835, 837–38 (1981) (stating that substantial-evidence standard used by North Carolina courts is equivalent to test announced in *Jackson*); State v. Rigsbee, 285 N.C. 708, 715–16, 208 S.E.2d 656, 661–62 (1974) (applying substantial-evidence standard to prosecution's proof of offense in case in which defendant also relied on entrapment defense); 1 BROUN, *supra* note 3, § 39, at 131 & n.92.

28. *See, e.g.*, *Rigsbee*, 285 N.C. at 715–16, 208 S.E.2d at 661–62. The court must also take into account evidence offered by the defendant that explains or clarifies the state's evidence as well as exculpatory features of the state's own evidence. *See* State v. Bates, 309 N.C. 528, 535, 308 S.E.2d 250, 262–63 (1983); State v. Bruton, 264 N.C. 488, 499, 142 S.E.2d 169, 176 (1965).

a rational trier of fact to conclude that the defendant had been induced to commit a crime that he or she was not predisposed to commit.[29]

The courts have recognized that entrapment is ordinarily a question of fact, for the jury to resolve; consequently, in the vast majority of cases they have refused to grant nonsuit.[30] Nevertheless, in some instances involving particularly strong evidence of entrapment, the courts have found entrapment as a matter of law.[31] In the cited cases, the courts dismissed the charges notwithstanding the presence of some evidence purportedly showing the defendant's predisposition, such as prior convictions unrelated to or remote in time from the current offense or acts committed after the current offense. The courts found the prosecution's evidence to be of such limited probative value that it was insufficient to overcome other, undisputed evidence of entrapment.

§ 6.3 JURY INSTRUCTIONS

(a) Giving of Instructions

A defendant who meets his or her burden of production on entrapment is entitled to have the jury instructed on the defense. Even in the absence of a request by the defendant, the trial court must instruct on the defense if the evidence introduced at trial supports the defense.[32]

---

29. *See* State v. Hageman, 307 N.C. 1, 30, 296 S.E.2d 433, 450 (1982); State v. Stanley, 288 N.C. 19, 32, 215 S.E.2d 589, 597 (1975). Technically, the burden of production shifts from the defendant to the prosecution when the defendant's evidence is strong enough to compel a finding of entrapment. If the prosecution fails to meet that burden, the defendant is entitled to entry of a verdict of acquittal. *See generally* 1 BROUN, *supra* note 3, § 34, at 120–23; 2 JOHN W. STRONG, MCCORMICK ON EVIDENCE § 338, at 419–21 (5th ed. 1999). As a practical matter, the court likely will not go through this burden-shifting analysis and will simply evaluate whether the evidence, considered as a whole, shows entrapment as a matter of law.

30. *See, e.g., Hageman*, 307 N.C. at 30–33, 296 S.E.2d at 450–51 (denying nonsuit); State v. Burnette, 242 N.C. 164, 169–73, 87 S.E.2d 191, 194–97 (1955); State v. Duncan, 75 N.C. App. 38, 46–47, 330 S.E.2d 481, 487–88 (1985); State v. Grier, 51 N.C. App. 209, 211–13, 275 S.E.2d 560, 562–63 (1981); State v. Dancy, 43 N.C. App. 208, 210–11, 258 S.E.2d 494, 495–96 (1979); State v. Braun, 31 N.C. App. 101, 102–03, 228 S.E.2d 466, 467 (1976); State v. Salame, 24 N.C. App. 1, 6–9, 210 S.E.2d 77, 81–83 (1974); State v. Williams, 14 N.C. App. 431, 432–33, 188 S.E.2d 717, 718 (1972).

31. *See, e.g.,* Jacobson v. United States, 503 U.S. 540 (1992) (solicitations over 2 1/2 year period); Sherman v. United States, 356 U.S. 369 (1958) (repeated solicitations to defendant to provide narcotics to informant, including appeals to alleviate informant's supposed suffering and inducements to defendant to return to own narcotics habit); *Stanley,* 288 N.C. 19, 215 S.E.2d 589 (28-year-old undercover police officer ingratiated himself into confidence and affection of 16 or 17-year-old defendant; opinion includes discussion of cases from other jurisdictions finding entrapment as matter of law); State v. Board, 296 N.C. 652, 252 S.E.2d 803 (1979) (three-judge plurality found insufficient evidence of elements of offense; three-judge concurrence would dismiss based on similarity to *Stanley*); United States v. Brooks, 215 F.3d 842 (8th Cir. 2000) (government informant supplied heroin to defendant, an addict, and then pressured him into selling it to undercover officer).

32. *See* State v. Sanders, 95 N.C. App. 56, 59–60, 381 S.E.2d 827, 829 (1989) (trial court erred in failing to instruct on entrapment, even though defendant did not object to court's instructions; however, failure to instruct is reviewed on appeal for plain error only).

In limited circumstances, the giving of entrapment instructions when not supported by the evidence may amount to error and warrant reversal of a conviction—for example, in cases in which the court gives an entrapment instruction not sought by the defendant and the instruction conflicts with the defendant's theory of defense.[33] In the typical case, however, the defendant has sought an entrapment instruction, so any error by the trial court in finding sufficient evidence for the instruction is favorable to the defendant and unlikely to be grounds for reversal.[34]

(b) Wording of Instructions

This section discusses the content of possible instructions in cases involving an entrapment defense; the discussion is not intended to be exhaustive.

Pattern Instructions. The pattern jury instruction on entrapment (issued by the Pattern Jury Committee, a committee composed of North Carolina superior court judges) has received the general approval of the appellate courts.[35] Because the instruction is generic in nature, however, trial courts may need to modify it to fit the case at hand.[36] Trial courts also must give the substance of instructions requested by the parties when the requested instructions are supported by the evidence and are a correct statement of the law.[37]

Meaning of Entrapment. The trial court must, of course, explain to the jury the essential concepts of entrapment—inducement and lack of predisposition. In some circumstances, however, more or less detail may be appropriate regarding one element or the other.

On the question of inducement, for example, the law requires that the inducement have come from a person acting on behalf of the government; therefore, as a general rule, the court should instruct the jury on this requirement. If, however, the evidence establishes conclusively

---

33. *See* State v. Tillman, 36 N.C. App. 141, 242 S.E.2d 898 (1978) (defendant was not relying on and presented no evidence of entrapment; instruction conflicted with defendant's theory of defense and required new trial); State v. Ransom, 2 N.C. App. 613, 163 S.E.2d 421 (1968) (to same effect); *compare* State v. Bland, 19 N.C. App. 560, 199 S.E.2d 497 (1973) (trial judge instructed on entrapment although not requested by defendant; giving of instruction did not prejudice defendant).

34. *See, e.g.,* State v. Kilgore, 246 N.C. 455, 456, 98 S.E.2d 346, 347 (1957) (record did not support entrapment defense; any error in jury charge was not prejudicial); State v. Rigsbee, 21 N.C. App. 188, 191–92, 203 S.E.2d 660, 663 (defendant received more beneficial instructions than he was entitled to have), *aff'd,* 285 N.C. 708, 716, 208 S.E.2d 656, 662 (1974).

35. *See* NORTH CAROLINA PATTERN JURY INSTRUCTIONS FOR CRIMINAL CASES (hereinafter N.C.P.I.—CRIM.) 309.10 (Dec. 1986); State v. Parker, 61 N.C. App. 585, 587, 301 S.E.2d 450, 451 (1983); State v. Gantt, 26 N.C. App. 554, 558, 217 S.E.2d 3, 6 (1975).

36. *See* N.C.P.I.—CRIM., *supra* note 35, at xix (June 2000) (cautioning that pattern instructions should be tailored to case as needed).

37. *See generally* State v. Rose, 323 N.C. 455, 458, 373 S.E.2d 426, 428 (1988); State v. Corn, 307 N.C. 79, 86, 296 S.E.2d 261, 266 (1982).

that the person was acting as a government agent, it may be inappropriate for the court to instruct the jury to decide the question of agency. Allowing the jury to do so would permit it to reject an entrapment defense on a ground not supported by the evidence.[38]

North Carolina cases have not considered how to deal with this problem. One possible approach would be for the trial court to instruct the jury that the undercover officer or informant was acting as an agent of the government. Such an instruction would amount to a partial directed verdict for the defendant, removing from the jury's consideration the issue of agency only; the jury would still have to decide whether the agent induced the defendant to commit a crime that he or she was not predisposed to commit.[39] Alternatively, the trial court could give a peremptory instruction on agency—that is, the court could instruct the jury that all the evidence shows that the undercover officer or informant was acting as an agent of the government and that, if the jury finds the facts to be as the evidence shows, it must find that the officer or informant was a government agent. Unlike a directed verdict, a peremptory instruction permits the jury to reject the evidence if it finds the evidence not credible.[40]

Variations in the instructions on predisposition may be necessary as well. For example, the United States Supreme Court has held that the defendant's predisposition to commit the offense must be measured as of the time the government initially approached the defendant, not when it actually solicited the defendant to commit the offense. This distinction may not be that significant if the solicitation to commit the crime occurred soon after the initial contact. It may be vital, however,

---

38. *Compare* United States v. Annese, 631 F.2d 1041, 1047–49 (1st Cir. 1980) (error for trial court to instruct on agency when undisputed facts showed that informant was agent of government) *with* United States v. Alzate, 70 F.3d 199, 200 (1st Cir. 1995) (defendant did not request different instruction on agency and was not prejudiced by trial court's failure to revise usual instruction); United States v. Fontenot, 14 F.3d 1364, 1369 (9th Cir. 1994) (no error for trial court to instruct jury to determine agency when facts were in dispute). For a discussion of agency principles, *see supra* § 2.4.

39. *See Annese*, 631 F.2d at 1047–49 (using this approach). The court may not direct a verdict, in whole or in part, in favor of the prosecution because doing so would invade the province of the jury. *See* 5 LaFave et al., *supra* note 9, § 24.6(b), at 541. But there is no constitutional prohibition on entry of a directed verdict in favor of the defendant, and the courts enter the equivalent of such verdicts by granting nonsuit. *See supra* § 6.2(c) note 31 and accompanying text (discussing cases finding entrapment as matter of law and granting nonsuit); *see also* State v. Temples, 74 N.C. App. 106, 109, 327 S.E.2d 266, 268 (1985) (in case involving self-defense, court holds that trial judge should not instruct jury to determine whether defendant was aggressor, a basis for rejecting the defense, if no evidence shows that defendant was aggressor).

40. This device is used in capital sentencing proceedings in North Carolina. The court must give a peremptory instruction on a mitigating circumstance if the uncontroverted evidence supports the circumstance; if the government stipulates to the mitigating circumstance, the court must give a mandatory peremptory instruction—that is, it must direct a verdict in the defendant's favor on that issue. *See* State v. Holden, 346 N.C. 404, 427–28, 488 S.E.2d 514, 526 (1997) (so holding).

if law enforcement officers engaged in an extended undercover operation against the defendant before proposing a criminal act. The instructions therefore may need to direct the jury to consider the defendant's predisposition before the government initially approached him or her.[41]

Good Character. In all criminal cases, the defendant is entitled, on request, to an instruction that the jury may consider evidence of the defendant's character for being law-abiding as evidence of his or her innocence of the crime charged. If a defendant offers such evidence in a case involving an entrapment defense, this instruction would be appropriate as well.[42]

Informants. If informants or undercover agents testify, the defendant may obtain an instruction on request about their potential bias.[43]

Burden of Proof. North Carolina law places on the defendant the burden of proving entrapment to the satisfaction of the jury. Commentators have suggested that jury instructions should contrast this standard with the higher, reasonable-doubt standard, and the pattern instruction on entrapment does this. Trying to define the standard further, however, may unduly confuse the jury.[44]

Final Mandate. The courts have required for some, although not all, defenses that the final mandate in jury instructions include as a possible verdict not guilty by reason of the particular defense—for example, not

41. *Compare* United States v. Lorenzo, 43 F.3d 1303, 1306–07 (9th Cir. 1995) (jury should be instructed to consider defendant's predisposition before encountering government agents) *with Alzate,* 70 F.3d at 200–01 (defendant did not request this revision; not plain error for trial court to give usual predisposition instruction). For a discussion of the potential significance of the timing of the government's contact with the defendant, *see supra* § 2.5(c).

42. *See* State v. Bogle, 324 N.C. 190, 199–200, 376 S.E.2d 745, 750 (1989) (stating general principle). Character traits, including the trait of being law-abiding, are ordinarily shown through opinion or reputation testimony. *See supra* § 5.2 (discussing use of reputation testimony in entrapment case). In entrapment cases, the defendant may also be able to offer evidence of specific good acts for the non-character purpose of showing lack of predisposition. *See supra* § 5.1(d) (discussing admissibility of such evidence); State v. Hageman, 307 N.C. 1, 25, 296 S.E.2d 433, 447 (1982) (expressing no opinion on whether defendant, on request, would be entitled to instruction to jury that such acts tend to negate predisposition to engage in criminal activity).

43. *See* N.C.P.I.—CRIM., *supra* note 35, at 104.30 (March 1986); State v. Wilkins, 34 N.C. App. 392, 398–99, 238 S.E.2d 659, 664 (1977) (court properly instructed jury on potential bias of undercover agent in entrapment case); *but cf.* State v. Clemmons, 100 N.C. App. 286, 293, 396 S.E.2d 616, 619 (1990) (although opinion suggests that defendant could rely on entrapment defense based on informant's actions on behalf of government, court finds that trial judge did not err in refusing to give instruction on potential bias of undercover agents and informants because informant was not in employ of police and did not receive any payment; court does not address possible inconsistency in its rulings).

44. *See* 1 BROUN, *supra* note 3, § 43, at 142–43 & n.168 (instructions contrasting "satisfaction" with "reasonable doubt" standard are clearly justified, but comparison to "preponderance" or "greater weight" may be confusing); State v. Franks, 300 N.C. 1, 17–18, 265 S.E.2d 177, 186–87 (1980) (instruction on defendant's burden to show insanity, which contrasted satisfaction and reasonable doubt standards but did not define satisfaction further, was adequate).

guilty by reason of self-defense.[45] The rationale for this requirement is that, without such a statement, the final mandate may unfairly emphasize verdicts favorable to the prosecution. The court of appeals has held that such a statement is not required (although not prohibited) when the defendant relies on entrapment.[46]

---

45. *Compare, e.g.,* State v. Buck, 310 N.C. 602, 607, 313 S.E.2d 550, 553–54 (1984) (required for self-defense) *with* State v. Pittman, 332 N.C. 244, 258–59, 420 S.E.2d 437, 445 (1992) (not required for diminished capacity).

46. *See* State v. Tate, 58 N.C. App. 494, 504–05, 294 S.E.2d 16, 22–23 (1982), *aff'd on other grounds,* 307 N.C. 464, 298 S.E.2d 386 (1983).

Table of Cases

The cases listed below are organized by jurisdiction (North Carolina, federal, and other states). Within each category the decisions are in alphabetical order.

NORTH CAROLINA CASES

State v. Adams, 115 N.C. 775, 20 S.E. 722 (1894), Ch. 3 nn.7, 14

State v. Addor, 183 N.C. 687, 110 S.E. 650 (1922), Ch. 3 n.22

State v. Alford, 289 N.C. 372, 222 S.E.2d 222, *vacated sub nom. on other grounds,* Carter v. North Carolina, 429 U.S. 809 (1976), Ch. 4 n.14

State v. Allison, 319 N.C. 92, 352 S.E.2d 420 (1987), Ch. 3 n.33

State v. Artis, 325 N.C. 278, 384 S.E.2d 470 (1989), *vacated on other grounds,* 494 U.S. 1023 (1990), Ch. 5 n.14

State v. Artis, 91 N.C. App. 604, 372 S.E.2d 905 (1988), Ch. 5 nn.8, 16

State v. Bailey, 93 N.C. App. 721, 379 S.E.2d 266 (1989), Ch. 2 nn.8, 37; Ch. 6 n.16

State v. Baldwin, 125 N.C. App. 530, 482 S.E.2d 1 (1997), Ch. 5 nn.52–53

State v. Bates, 309 N.C. 528, 308 S.E.2d 258 (1983), Ch. 6 n.28

State v. Blackwell, 67 N.C. App. 432, 313 S.E.2d 797 (1984), Ch. 2 nn.44, 83; Ch. 6 n.15

State v. Bland, 19 N.C. App. 560, 199 S.E.2d 497 (1973), Ch. 6 n.33

State v. Board, 296 N.C. 652, 252 S.E.2d 803 (1979), Ch. 2 n.40; Ch. 6 n.31

State v. Bogle, 324 N.C. 190, 376 S.E.2d 745 (1989), Ch. 5 nn.34, 45–46; Ch. 6 n.42

State v. Boles, 246 N.C. 83, 97 S.E.2d 476 (1957), Ch. 4 nn.25–26

State v. Booher, 305 N.C. 554, 290 S.E.2d 561 (1982), Ch. 3 nn.2, 4, 6, 9, 12, 14

State v. Boone, 297 N.C. 652, 256 S.E.2d 683 (1979), Ch. 3 n.8

State v. Bradshaw, 12 N.C. App. 510, 183 S.E.2d 787 (1971), Ch. 2 nn.44, 49; Ch. 6 n.15

State v. Braun, 31 N.C. App. 101, 228 S.E.2d 466 (1976), Ch. 2 n.41; Ch. 4 n.26; Ch. 6 nn.22, 30

State v. Brockenborough, 45 N.C. App. 121, 262 S.E.2d 330 (1980), Ch. 4 n.8; Ch. 5 n.48

State v. Broome, 136 N.C. App. 82, 523 S.E.2d 448 (1999), Ch. 1 n.7; Ch. 5 n.33

State v. Bruton, 264 N.C. 488, 142 S.E.2d 169 (1965), Ch. 6 n.28

State v. Bryant, 334 N.C. 333, 432 S.E.2d 291 (1993), *vacated on other grounds,* 511 U.S. 1001 (1994), Ch. 6 n.19

State v. Bryant, 251 N.C. 217, 110 S.E.2d 892 (1959), Ch. 2 n.4

State v. Buck, 310 N.C. 602, 313 S.E.2d 550 (1984), Ch. 6 n.45

State v. Burnette, 242 N.C. 164, 87 S.E.2d 191 (1955), Ch. 2 nn.13, 19, 29, 35, 61; Ch. 3 nn.6, 13; Ch. 4 n.31; Ch. 6 nn.14, 30

State v. Caldwell, 249 N.C. 56, 105 S.E.2d 189 (1958), Ch. 2 nn.1, 13, 30, 49; Ch. 3 n.42

State v. Cheek, 351 N.C. 48, 520 S.E.2d 545 (1999), Ch. 4 n.7

State v. Clark, 324 N.C. 146, 377 S.E.2d 54 (1989), Ch. 6 nn.11–13, 107

State v. Clark, 137 N.C. App. 90, 527 S.E.2d 319 (2000), Ch. 3 n.24

State v. Clemmons, 100 N.C. App. 286, 396 S.E.2d 616 (1990), Ch. 1 n.7; Ch. 2 n.51; Ch. 6 n.43

State v. Coble, 351 N.C. 448, 527 S.E.2d 45 (2000), Ch. 3 n.22

State v. Coffey, 326 N.C. 268, 389 S.E.2d 48 (1990), Ch. 5 n.2

State v. Coleman, 270 N.C. 357, 154 S.E.2d 485 (1967), Ch. 2 n.35; Ch. 3 n.9

State v. Collins, 345 N.C. 170, 478 S.E.2d 191 (1996), Ch. 5 n.46

State v. Cook, 263 N.C. 730, 140 S.E.2d 305 (1965), Ch. 6 n.5

State v. Corn, 307 N.C. 79, 296 S.E.2d 261 (1982), Ch. 6 n.37

State v. Crawford, 104 N.C. App. 591, 410 S.E.2d 499 (1991), Ch. 5 n.43

State v. Dancy, 43 N.C. App. 208, 258 S.E.2d 494 (1979), Ch. 5 n.23; Ch. 6 n.30

State v. Davis, 126 N.C. App. 415, 485 S.E.2d 329 (1997), Ch. 1 n.7

State v. Davis, 38 N.C. App. 672, 248 S.E.2d 883 (1978), Ch. 2 n.29

State v. DeLeonardo, 315 N.C. 762, 340 S.E.2d 350 (1986), Ch. 5 n.4

State v. Demott, 26 N.C. App. 14, 214 S.E.2d 781 (1975), Ch. 2 n.9

State v. Duncan, 75 N.C. App. 38, 330 S.E.2d 481 (1985), Ch. 2 nn.34, 82; Ch. 6 n.30

State v. Emery, 91 N.C. App. 24, 370 S.E.2d 456 (1988), Ch. 5 n.20

State v. Fields, 324 N.C. 204, 376 S.E.2d 740 (1989), Ch. 6 nn.13, 19

State v. Flannigan, 78 N.C. App. 629, 338 S.E.2d 109 (1985), Ch. 5 n.9

State v. Fletcher, 279 N.C. 85, 181 S.E.2d 405 (1971), Ch. 2 nn.13, 37; Ch. 4 n.6

State v. Forrest, 321 N.C. 186, 362 S.E.2d 252 (1987), Ch. 3 n.11

State v. Franks, 300 N.C. 1, 265 S.E.2d 177 (1980), Ch. 6 n.44

State v. Gantt, 26 N.C. App. 554, 217 S.E.2d 3 (1975), Ch. 6 n.35

State v. Garner, 330 N.C. 273, 410 S.E.2d 861 (1991), Ch. 5 n.21

State v. Gay, 334 N.C. 467, 434 S.E.2d 840 (1993), Ch. 5 n.52

State v. Godwin, 227 N.C. 449, 42 S.E.2d 617 (1947), Ch. 1 n.4

State v. Goffney, 157 N.C. 624, 73 S.E. 162 (1911), Ch. 3 n.8

State v. Goldman, 97 N.C. App. 589, 389 S.E.2d 281 (1990), Ch. 5 nn.3, 18, 20, 23, 40

State v. Gooding, 196 N.C. 710, 146 S.E. 806 (1929), Ch. 3 n.10

State v. Gordon, 104 N.C. App. 455, 410 S.E.2d 4 (1991), Ch. 5 n.20

State v. Grainger, 60 N.C. App. 188, 298 S.E.2d 203 (1982), Ch. 4 nn.4, 6

State v. Green, 27 N.C. App. 491, 219 S.E.2d 529 (1975), Ch. 2 n.8

State v. Grier, 51 N.C. App. 209, 275 S.E.2d 560 (1981), Ch. 2 n.41; Ch. 6 n.30

State v. Gunnings, 122 N.C. App. 294, 468 S.E.2d 613 (1996), Ch. 3 nn.22, 25

State v. Hageman, 307 N.C. 1, 296 S.E.2d 433 (1982), Ch. 1 nn.6, 8; Ch. 2 nn.3, 19, 46, 48, 61, 67, 79; Ch. 3 nn.19–20, 22; Ch. 4 n.31; Ch. 5 nn.27, 36, 46, 54; Ch. 6 nn.7, 29–30, 42

State v. Hankerson, 288 N.C. 632, 220 S.E.2d 575 (1975), *rev'd on other grounds,* 432 U.S. 233 (1977), Ch. 6 n.6

State v. Harris, 21 N.C. App. 697, 205 S.E.2d 336 (1974), Ch. 2 n.51

State v. Hartman, 49 N.C. App. 83, 270 S.E.2d 609 (1980), Ch. 2 n.41

State v. Hendrix, 19 N.C. App. 99, 197 S.E.2d 892 (1973), Ch. 2 n.17

State v. Hodges, 51 N.C. App. 229, 275 S.E.2d 533 (1981), Ch. 4 nn.5, 9

State v. Holden, 346 N.C. 404, 488 S.E.2d 514 (1997), Ch. 6 n.40

State v. Hopkins, 154 N.C. 622, 70 S.E. 394 (1911), Ch. 1 n.1

State v. Hughes, 208 N.C. 542, 181 S.E. 737 (1935), Ch. 1 n.4; Ch. 3 n.5, 7–8, 14

State v. Hunt, 283 N.C. 617, 197 S.E.2d 513 (1973), Ch. 4 n.18

State v. Ice & Fuel Co., 166 N.C. 366, 81 S.E. 737 (1914), Ch. 1 n.1

State v. Jackson, 243 N.C. 216, 90 S.E.2d 507 (1955), Ch. 2 nn.45, 50, 55; Ch. 6 n.16

State v. Jamerson, 64 N.C. App. 301, 307 S.E.2d 436 (1983), Ch. 2 nn.41, 67, 83; Ch. 5 n.37; Ch. 6 n.15

State v. Jernagan, 4 N.C. 483 (1817), Ch. 3 n.7

State v. Johnson, 81 N.C. App. 454, 344 S.E.2d 318 (1986), Ch. 4 n.4

State v. Jones, 303 N.C. 500, 279 S.E.2d 835 (1981), Ch. 6 n.27

State v. Keen, 25 N.C. App. 567, 214 S.E.2d 242 (1975), Ch. 3 n.17

State v. Kilgore, 246 N.C. 455, 98 S.E.2d 346 (1957), Ch. 2 n.34; Ch. 6 n.34

State v. Lea, 126 N.C. App. 440, 485 S.E.2d 874 (1997), Ch. 3 n.22

State v. Logan, 79 N.C. App. 420, 339 S.E.2d 449 (1986), Ch. 4 n.8

State v. Love, 229 N.C. 99, 47 S.E.2d 712 (1948), Ch. 1 nn.5–6; Ch. 2 nn.6, 29

State v. Luster, 306 N.C. 566, 295 S.E.2d 421 (1982), Ch. 2 nn.3, 20, 58–59, 70; Ch. 4 nn.24, 28–29; Ch. 6 nn.14, 24

State v. Martin, 77 N.C. App. 61, 334 S.E.2d 459 (1985), Ch. 2 n.34; Ch. 6 n.16

State v. Mash, 323 N.C. 339, 372 S.E.2d 532 (1988), Ch. 6 nn.21–22

State v. McAuliffe, 22 N.C. App. 601, 207 S.E.2d 1 (1974), Ch. 4 n.6

State v. McCaslin, 132 N.C. App. 352, 511 S.E.2d 347 (1999), Ch. 1 n.7; Ch. 2 n.8

State v. McEachern, 114 N.C. App. 218, 441 S.E.2d 574 (1994), Ch. 4 n.10

State v. McGee, 60 N.C. App. 658, 299 S.E.2d 796 (1983), Ch. 2 n.56

State v. Moctezuma, 141 N.C. App. __, 539 S.E.2d 52 (2000), Ch. 4 n.7

State v. Moore, 41 N.C. App. 148, 254 S.E.2d 252 (1979), Ch. 5 n.50

State v. Murrell, 54 N.C. App. 342, 283 S.E.2d 173 (1981), Ch. 2 n.17

State v. Nelson, 232 N.C. 602, 61 S.E.2d 626 (1950), Ch. 3 nn.6, 10

State v. Neville, 302 N.C. 623, 276 S.E.2d 373 (1981), Ch. 4 nn.18, 23, 26–27, 32

State v. Newkirk, 73 N.C. App. 83, 325 S.E.2d 518 (1985), Ch. 4 n.8

State v. Orr, 28 N.C. App. 317, 220 S.E.2d 848 (1976), Ch. 4 n.5

State v. Paige, 316 N.C. 630, 343 S.E.2d 848 (1986), Ch. 4 n.14

State v. Parker, 137 N.C. App. 590, 530 S.E.2d 297 (2000), Ch. 3 n.52

State v. Parker, 61 N.C. App. 585, 301 S.E.2d 450 (1983), Ch. 4 n.5; Ch. 6 nn.5, 35

State v. Payne, 337 N.C. 505, 448 S.E.2d 93 (1994), Ch. 6 n.6

State v. Pickens, 335 N.C. 717, 440 S.E.2d 552 (1994), Ch. 4 n.11

State v. Pittman, 332 N.C. 244, 420 S.E.2d 437 (1992), Ch. 6 n.45

State v. Ransom, 2 N.C. App. 613, 163 S.E.2d 421 (1968), Ch. 6 n.33

State v. Rigsbee, 285 N.C. 708, 208 S.E.2d 656 (1974), Ch. 6 nn.27–28

State v. Rigsbee, 21 N.C. App. 188, 203 S.E.2d 660, aff'd, 285 N.C. 708, 208 S.E.2d 656 (1974), Ch. 6 n.34

State v. Rosario, 93 N.C. App. 627, 379 S.E.2d 434 (1989), Ch. 2 n.36; Ch. 3 nn.16, 23, 41, 57; Ch. 4 n.31; Ch. 5 n.3; Ch. 6 n.16

State v. Rose, 323 N.C. 455, 373 S.E.2d 426 (1988), Ch. 6 n.37

State v. Ross, 329 N.C. 108, 405 S.E.2d 158 (1991), Ch. 6 n.2

State v. Salame, 24 N.C. App. 1, 210 S.E.2d 77 (1974), Ch. 2 nn.38, 59; Ch. 3 nn.41, 45; Ch. 5 nn.17, 23; Ch. 6 n.30

State v. Sanders, 95 N.C. App. 56, 381 S.E.2d 827 (1989), Ch. 2 nn.42, 49, 60, 65; Ch. 4 nn.25, 29; Ch. 6 nn.15, 32

State v. Sexton, 336 N.C. 321, 444 S.E.2d 879 (1994), Ch. 5 n.42

State v. Simmons, 65 N.C. App. 294, 309 S.E.2d 493 (1983), Ch. 4 n.13

State v. Smith, 300 N.C. 71, 265 S.E.2d 164 (1980), Ch. 6 nn.20–21

State v. Smith, 152 N.C. 798, 67 S.E. 508 (1910), Ch. 1 n.1; Ch. 3 n.7

State v. Squire, 321 N.C. 541, 364 S.E.2d 354 (1988), Ch. 5 n.46

State v. Stanback, 19 N.C. App. 375, 198 S.E.2d 759 (1973), Ch. 2 n.34; Ch. 6 n.16

State v. Stanley, 288 N.C. 19, 215 S.E.2d 589 (1975), Ch. 1 n.5; Ch. 2 nn.2, 39–40, 61, 70, 77, 82, 87; Ch. 5 nn.18, 37; Ch. 6 nn.29, 31

State v. Swaney, 277 N.C. 602, 178 S.E.2d 399 (1971), Ch. 4 n. 25

State v. Tate, 58 N.C. App. 494, 294 S.E.2d 16 (1982), *aff'd on other grounds*, 307 N.C. 464, 298 S.E.2d 386 (1983), Ch. 4 n.9; Ch. 6 n.46

State v. Taylor, 117 N.C. App. 644, 453 S.E.2d 225 (1995), Ch. 5 n.46

State v. Temples, 74 N.C. App. 106, 327 S.E.2d 266 (1985), Ch. 6 n.39

State v. Thomas, 52 N.C. App. 186, 278 S.E.2d 535 (1981), Ch. 2 n.51; Ch. 6 n.16

State v. Thompson, 142 N.C. App. __ , 543 S.E.2d 160 (2001), Ch. 1 n.7; Ch. 2 n.82

State v. Tillman, 36 N.C. App. 141, 242 S.E.2d 898 (1978), Ch. 3 n.30; Ch. 6 n.33

State v. Todd, 264 N.C. 524, 142 S.E.2d 154 (1965), Ch. 4 n.37

State v. Turner, 66 N.C. App. 203, 311 S.E.2d 331 (1984), Ch. 5 n.46

State v. Vestal, 131 N.C. App. 756, 509 S.E.2d 249 (1998), Ch. 3 n.49

State v. Wagoner, 249 N.C. 637, 107 S.E.2d 83 (1959), Ch. 4 n.37

State v. Walker, 295 N.C. 510, 246 S.E.2d 748 (1978), Ch. 2 nn.30, 33, 60; Ch. 6 nn.14, 16

State v. Walker, 251 N.C. 465, 112 S.E.2d 61 (1960), Ch. 3 nn.15–16

State v. Walker, 66 N.C. App. 367, 311 S.E.2d 329 (1984), Ch. 2 n.44; Ch. 6 nn.15, 21

State v. Wallace, 246 N.C. 445, 98 S.E.2d 473 (1957), Ch. 2 nn.1, 6

State v. Watson, 303 N.C. 533, 279 S.E.2d 580 (1981), Ch. 4 n.7

State v. Whisnant, 36 N.C. App. 252, 243 S.E.2d 395 (1978), Ch. 1 n.6; Ch. 2 nn.43, 45, 57; Ch. 6 n.15

State v. White, 135 N.C. App. 349, 520 S.E.2d 70 (1999), Ch. 5 n.14

State v. Wilkins, 34 N.C. App. 392, 238 S.E.2d 659 (1977), Ch. 3 nn.15–16, 30; Ch. 6 n.43

State v. Williams, 14 N.C. App. 431, 188 S.E.2d 717 (1972), Ch. 6 n.30

State v. Willis, 136 N.C. App. 820, 526 S.E.2d 191 (2000), Ch. 5 n.11

State v. Wooten, 55 N.C. App. 530, 286 S.E.2d 635 (1982), Ch. 2 n.17

State v. Worthington, 84 N.C. App. 150, 352 S.E.2d 695 (1987), Ch. 5 n.48

State v. Yost, 9 N.C. App. 671, 177 S.E.2d 320 (1970), Ch. 4 n.27

FEDERAL CASES

Apprendi v. New Jersey, 530 U.S. 466 (2000), Ch. 3 n.55; Ch. 6 n.4

Capps v. Sullivan, 921 F.2d 260 (10th Cir. 1990), Ch. 1 n.14

Cox v. Louisiana, 379 U.S. 559 (1965), Ch. 3 n.26

De Jong v. United States, 381 F.2d 725 (9th Cir. 1967), Ch. 5 n.19

Eaglin v. Welborn, 57 F.3d 496 (7th Cir. 1995), Ch. 4 n.34

Hampton v. United States, 425 U.S. 484 (1976), Ch. 1 n.12; Ch.2 n.20; Ch. 3 nn.35, 38

In re Winship, 397 U.S. 358 (1970), Ch. 6 n.4

Jackson v. Virginia, 443 U.S. 307 (1979), Ch. 6 n.27

Jacobson v. United States, 503 U.S. 540 (1992), Ch. 1 n.12; Ch. 2 nn.72, 84–85; Ch. 6 n.31

Kyles v. Whitley, 514 U.S. 419 (1995), Ch. 4 n.3

Lopez v. United States, 373 U.S. 427 (1963), Ch. 1 n.12

Masciale v. United States, 356 U.S. 386 (1958), Ch. 1 n.12

Mathews v. United States, 485 U.S. 58 (1988), Ch. 1 n.12; Ch. 4 nn.17, 33

McCray v. Illinois, 386 U.S. 300 (1967), Ch. 4 n.3

McLawhorn v. North Carolina, 484 F.2d 1 (4th Cir. 1973), *vacating* 16 N.C. App. 153, 191 S.E.2d 410 (1972), Ch. 2 n.39; Ch. 4 n.5

Montana v. Egelhoff, 518 U.S. 37 (1996), Ch. 6 n.10

Mullaney v. Wilbur, 421 U.S. 684 (1975), Ch. 6 n.4

Ornelas v. United States, 517 U.S. 690 (1996), Ch. 3 n.52

Osborn v. United States, 385 U.S. 323 (1966), Ch. 1 n.12

Raley v. Ohio, 360 U.S. 423 (1959), Ch. 3 n.26

Roviaro v. United States, 353 U.S. 53 (1957), Ch. 4 nn.2–3, 10

Sherman v. United States, 356 U.S. 369 (1958), Ch. 1 n.12; Ch. 2 nn.23, 39, 49, 77; Ch. 6 n.31

Sorrells v. United States, 287 U.S. 435 (1932), Ch. 1 nn.2–3, 12; Ch. 2 nn.12, 22; Ch. 3 n.2; Ch. 5 n.1

United States v. Abcasis, 45 F.3d 39 (2d Cir. 1995), Ch. 3 n.29

United States v. Achter, 52 F.3d 753 (8th Cir. 1995), Ch. 3 nn.27, 31

United States v. Al-Talib, 55 F.3d 923 (4th Cir. 1995), Ch. 2 n.17

United States v. Alzate, 70 F.3d 199 (1st Cir. 1995), Ch. 6 nn.38, 41

United States v. Angle, 230 F.3d 113 (4th Cir. 2000), Ch. 3 n.55

United States v. Annese, 631 F.2d 1041 (1st Cir. 1980), Ch. 4 n.21; Ch. 6 nn.38–39

United States v. Aquino-Chacon, 109 F.3d 936 (4th Cir. 1997), Ch. 3 n.27

United States v. Baptista-Rodriguez, 17 F.3d 1354 (11th Cir. 1994), Ch. 3 nn.27, 31, 33

United States v. Barth, 990 F.2d 422 (8th Cir. 1993), Ch. 3 n.54

United States v. Batres-Santolino, 521 F. Supp. 744 (N.D. Cal. 1981), Ch. 3 n.46

United States v. Becerra, 992 F.2d 960 (9th Cir. 1993), Ch. 6 n.19

United States v. Blankenship, 775 F.2d 735 (6th Cir. 1985), Ch. 5 nn.12, 14

United States v. Boyd, 55 F.3d 239 (7th Cir. 1995), Ch. 3 n.36

United States v. Branham, 97 F.3d 835 (6th Cir. 1996), Ch. 5 nn.49–50

United States v. Brooks, 215 F.3d 842 (8th Cir. 2000), Ch. 5 n. 23; Ch. 6. n. 31

United States v. Burkley, 591 F.2d 903 (D.C. Cir. 1978), Ch. 5 n.5

United States v. Cannon, 886 F. Supp. 705 (D.N.D. 1995), rev'd on other grounds, 88 F.3d 1495 (8th Cir. 1996), Ch. 2 n.11: Ch. 3 n.54

United States v. Casanova, 970 F.2d 371 (7th Cir. 1992), Ch. 5 n.23

United States v. Cunningham, 529 F.2d 884 (6th Cir. 1976), Ch. 5 n.9

United States v. Daniels, 572 F.2d 535 (5th Cir. 1978), Ch. 5 n.20

United States v. DeVore, 423 F.2d 1069 (4th Cir. 1970), Ch. 2 n.32

United States v. Dove, 629 F.2d 325 (4th Cir. 1980), Ch. 3 n.19

United States v. Duncan, 896 F.2d 271 (7th Cir. 1990), Ch. 3 n.44

United States v. Fadel, 844 F.2d 1425 (10th Cir. 1988), Ch. 2 n.16

United States v. Fontenot, 14 F.3d 1364 (9th Cir. 1994), Ch. 6 n.38

United States v. Garcia, 79 F.3d 74 (7th Cir. 1996), Ch. 3 n.55

United States v. Gendron, 18 F.3d 955 (1st Cir. 1994), Ch. 2 nn.31, 73

United States v. Hollingsworth, 27 F.3d 1196 (7th Cir. 1994), Ch. 2 nn.45, 53, 66, 71, 83

United States v. Hunt, 749 F.2d 1078 (4th Cir. 1984), Ch.2 n.20; Ch. 5 nn.26, 32

United States v. Jiminez, 613 F.2d 1373 (5th Cir. 1980), Ch. 5 n.23

United States v. Jones, 18 F.3d 1145 (4th Cir. 1994), Ch. 3 n.53

United States v. Jones, 976 F.2d 176 (4th Cir. 1992), Ch. 2 n.79

United States v. Knox, 112 F.3d 802 (5th Cir. 1997), rev'd sub nom. on other grounds, United States v. Brace, 145 F.3d 247 (5th Cir. 1998), Ch. 2 n.73

United States v. Lewis, 53 F.3d 29 (4th Cir. 1995), Ch. 3 n.15

United States v. Lorenzo, 43 F.3d 1303 (9th Cir. 1995), Ch. 6 n.41

United States v. Manzella, 791 F.2d 1263 (7th Cir. 1986), Ch. 2 n.45

United States v. Mason, 902 F.2d 1434 (9th Cir. 1990), Ch. 3 nn.31, 33

United States v. McClain, 531 F.2d 431 (9th Cir. 1976), Ch. 5 nn.26, 30

United States v. McClelland, 72 F.3d 717 (9th Cir. 1995), Ch. 3 n.58

United States v. Montgomery, 998 F.2d 1468 (9th Cir. 1993), Ch. 4 n.8

United States v. Montilla, 870 F.2d 549 (9th Cir. 1989), amended on other grounds, 907 F.2d 115 (9th Cir. 1990), Ch. 3 n.49

United States v. Mulherin, 710 F.2d 731 (11th Cir. 1983), Ch. 4 n.12

United States v. Navarro, 737 F.2d 625 (7th Cir. 1984), Ch. 2 n.66, 82; Ch. 5 n.38

United States v. Newman, 849 F.2d 156 (5th Cir. 1988), Ch. 5 n.51

United States v. Nixon, 777 F.2d 958 (5th Cir. 1985), Ch. 5 n.29

United States v. Nunn, 940 F.2d 1148 (8th Cir. 1991), Ch. 5 n.51

United States v. Osborne, 935 F.2d 32 (4th Cir. 1991), Ch. 3 n.39

United States v. Pitt, 193 F.3d 751 (3d Cir. 1999), Ch. 3 n.44

United States v. Price, 783 F.2d 1132 (4th Cir. 1986), Ch. 4 n.4

United States v. Quinn, 543 F.2d 640 (8th Cir. 1976), Ch. 3 n.43

United States v. Richardson, 764 F.2d 1514 (11th Cir. 1985), Ch. 5 nn.6, 44, 46

United States v. Ricks, 882 F.2d 885 (4th Cir. 1989), Ch. 4 n.12

United States v. Rogers, 121 F.3d 12 (1st Cir. 1997), Ch. 5 n.24

United States v. Russell, 411 U.S. 423 (1973), Ch. 1 n.12; Ch. 3 n.34

United States v. Sarihifard, 155 F.3d 301 (4th Cir. 1998), Ch. 2 n.5

United States v. Scott, 437 U.S. 82 (1978), Ch. 3 n.49

United States v. Shephard, 4 F.3d 647 (8th Cir. 1993), Ch. 3 n.56

United States v. Stanley, 765 F.2d 1224 (5th Cir. 1985), Ch. 3 n.43

United States v. Stauffer, 38 F.3d 1103 (9th Cir. 1994), Ch. 3 n.54

United States v. Stavig, 80 F.3d 1241 (8th Cir. 1996), Ch. 3 n.55

United States v. Thickstun, 110 F.3d 1394 (9th Cir. 1997), Ch. 2 n.73

United States v. Thomas, 134 F.3d 975 (9th Cir. 1998), Ch. 5 n.35

United States v. Tucker, 28 F.3d 1420 (6th Cir. 1994), Ch. 3 n.36

United States v. Twigg, 588 F.2d 373 (3d Cir. 1978), Ch. 3 n.39

United States v. Valencia, 645 F.2d 1158 (2d Cir. 1980), Ch. 4 n.22

United States v. Webster, 649 F.2d 346 (5th Cir. 1981), Ch. 5 nn.28–32, 40, 46–47

United States v. West Indies Transp., Inc., 127 F.3d 299 (3d Cir. 1997), Ch. 3 n.29

United States v. Williams, 644 F.2d 950 (2d Cir. 1981), Ch. 3 n.47

OTHER STATE CASES

Commonwealth v. Monteagudo, 693 N.E.2d 1381 (Mass. 1998), Ch. 3 n.43

Foster v. State, 13 P.3d 61 (Nev. 2000), Ch. 2 n.79

Hopson v. State, 625 So. 2d 395 (Miss. 1993), Ch. 4 n.35

Kent v. State, 704 So. 2d 121 (Fla. Dist. Ct. App. 1997), Ch. 2 n.67; Ch. 5 nn.37, 50

Lambeth v. State, 562 So. 2d 575 (Ala. 1990), Ch. 5 n.26

Melton v. State, 713 S.W.2d 107 (Tex. Crim. App. 1986), Ch. 4 n.22

Metcalf v. State, 635 So. 2d 11 (Fla. 1994), Ch. 3 n.40

People v. Placek, 704 N.E.2d 393 (Ill. 1998), Ch. 5 n.19

People v. Shine, 590 N.Y.S.2d 965 (N.Y. App. Div. 1992), Ch. 3 n.40

Shrader v. State, 706 P.2d 834 (Nev. 1985), Ch. 2 n.79

State v. Gibbons, 519 A.2d 350 (N.J. 1987), Ch. 5 nn.15, 18–19

State v. Glosson, 462 So. 2d 1082 (Fla. 1985), Ch. 3 n.40

State v. Lively, 921 P.2d 1035 (Wash. 1996), Ch. 3 n.40

State v. Preston, 4 P.3d 1004 (Ariz. Ct. App. 2000), Ch. 4 n.20

State v. Soule, 811 P.2d 1071 (Ariz. 1991), Ch. 4 n.20

Stripling v. State, 349 So. 2d 187 (Fla. Dist. Ct. App. 1977), Ch. 4 n.31

Sykes v. State, 739 So. 2d 641 (Fla. Dist. Ct. App. 1999), Ch. 5 n.35

Table of Statutes and Rules

Statutes and rules appear in either the text or footnotes of the cited sections.

NORTH CAROLINA STATUTES

N.C. Gen. Stat. 15A-405, § 3.2(b)
N.C. Gen. Stat. 15A-903(a)(2), § 4.1
N.C. Gen. Stat. 15A-927(c)(2), § 4.2
N.C. Gen. Stat. 15A-952, § 3.3(b)
N.C. Gen. Stat. 15A-952(f), § 3.3(b)
N.C. Gen. Stat. 15A-959(a), § 6.1
N.C. Gen. Stat. 15A-959(b), § 5.4, § 6.1
N.C. Gen. Stat. 15A-978(b), § 4.1

N.C. Gen. Stat. 15A-979(b), § 3.3(b)
N.C. Gen. Stat. 15A-1340.13(g), § 3.4
N.C. Gen. Stat. 15A-1340.13(h), § 3.4
N.C. Gen. Stat. 15A-1340.16(e), § 3.4
N.C. Gen. Stat. 15A-1340.16(e)(1), § 3.4
N.C. Gen. Stat. 15A-1444(e), § 3.3(b)
N.C. Gen. Stat. 15A-1445, § 3.3(b)
N.C. Gen. Stat. 90-101(c)(5), § 3.2(b)

NORTH CAROLINA RULES OF EVIDENCE

N.C. R. Evid. 403, § 5.1(b), (c)
N.C. R. Evid. 404(a)(1), § 5.2
N.C. R. Evid. 404(b), § 5.1, § 5.2
N.C. R. Evid. 405, § 5.2
N.C. R. Evid. 405(a), § 5.4
N.C. R. Evid. 405(b), § 5.1(a)
N.C. R. Evid. 608, § 5.2

N.C. R. Evid. 608(b), § 5.1(a)
N.C. R. Evid. 609, § 5.1(b), § 5.2
N.C. R. Evid. 702, § 5.4
N.C. R. Evid. 801(d), § 5.3
N.C. R. Evid. 803(3), § 5.3
N.C. R. Evid. 803(21), § 5.2

OTHER RULES

N.C. R. App. P. 21(a)(1), § 3.3(b)
Fed. R. Crim. P. 11(a)(2), § 3.3(b)

Fed. R. Crim. P. 12(b), § 3.3(b)
Fed. R. Evid., § 5.1(a)

References

Books

BROUN, KENNETH S., BRANDIS AND BROUN ON NORTH CAROLINA EVIDENCE (5th ed. 1998).

FARB, ROBERT L., ARREST, SEARCH, AND INVESTIGATION (Institute of Government, 2d ed. 1992).

————, NORTH CAROLINA CRIMES: A GUIDEBOOK ON THE ELEMENTS OF CRIME (Institute of Government, 5th ed. 2001).

HORN, CARL, FOURTH CIRCUIT CRIMINAL HANDBOOK: 2001 EDITION (2000).

LAFAVE, WAYNE R., ET AL., CRIMINAL PROCEDURE (2d ed. 1999).

LAFAVE, WAYNE R. & AUSTIN W. SCOTT, JR., SUBSTANTIVE CRIMINAL LAW (1986).

MARCUS, PAUL, THE ENTRAPMENT DEFENSE (2d ed. 1995).

MODEL PENAL CODE AND COMMENTARIES (1985).

MOSTELLER, ROBERT P., ET AL., NORTH CAROLINA EVIDENTIARY FOUNDATIONS (1998).

NORTH CAROLINA PATTERN JURY INSTRUCTIONS FOR CRIMINAL CASES (2000).

PERKINS, ROLLIN M. & RONALD N. BOYCE, CRIMINAL LAW (3d ed. 1982).

ROBINSON, PAUL H., CRIMINAL LAW DEFENSES (1984).

RUBIN, JOHN, THE LAW OF SELF-DEFENSE IN NORTH CAROLINA (Institute of Government, 1996).

STRONG, JOHN W., MCCORMICK ON EVIDENCE (4th ed. 1992).

WRIGHT, CHARLES ALAN & KENNETH W. GRAHAM, JR., FEDERAL PRACTICE AND PROCEDURE (1978).

Articles

Allen, Ronald J., *Structuring Jury Decisionmaking in Criminal Cases: A Unified Constitutional Approach to Evidentiary Devices,* 94 HARV. L. REV. 321 (1980).

Bennett, Fred Warren, *From* Sorrells *to* Jacobson: *Reflections on Six Decades of Entrapment Law, and Related Defenses, in Federal Court,* 27 WAKE FOREST L. REV. 829 (1992).

Coates, Albert, *Limitations on Investigating Officers,* 15 N.C. L. REV. 229 (1936–37).

Connelly, Sean, *Bad Advice: The Entrapment by Estoppel Doctrine in Criminal Law,* 48 U. MIAMI L. REV. 627 (1994).

Dellinger, Anne, *How We Die in North Carolina,* POPULAR GOV'T, Spring 1999.

Hardy, Ben A., *The Traps of Entrapment,* 3 AM. J. CRIM. L. 165 (1974).

Hastings, Karis A., Note, *Entrapment and Denial of the Crime: A Defense of the Inconsistency Rule,* 1986 DUKE L.J. 866 (1986).

Hicks, George Robert, III, Note, 11 CAMPBELL L. REV. 279 (1989).

Johnson, W. H., III, *Proving a Criminal Predisposition: Separating the Unwary Innocent from the Unwary Criminal*, 43 DUKE L.J. 384 (1993).

Marcus, Paul, *Presenting, Back from the [Almost] Dead, the Entrapment Defense*, 47 FLA. L. REV. 205 (1995).

Miller, Stephen A., Comment, *The Case for Preserving the Outrageous Government Conduct Defense*, 91 NW. U. L. REV. 305 (1996).

Note, *Entrapment Through Unsuspecting Middlemen*, 95 HARV. L. REV. 1122 (1982).

Rubin, John, *The Diminished Capacity Defense*, ADMINISTRATION OF JUSTICE MEMORANDUM No. 92/01 (Institute of Government, 1992).

———, *The Voluntary Intoxication Defense*, ADMINISTRATION OF JUSTICE MEMORANDUM No. 93/01 (Institute of Government, 1993).

Rubin, John & Ben F. Loeb, Jr., *Punishments for North Carolina Crimes and Motor Vehicle Offenses: 2000 Cumulative Supplement*, ADMINISTRATION OF JUSTICE BULLETIN No. 2000/04 (Institute of Government, 2000).

A.L.R. ANNOTATIONS

Bock, J. A., *Entrapment to Commit Offense against Obscenity Laws*, 77 A.L.R.2d 792 (1961).

Buckner, D. E., *Entrapment to Commit Bribery or Offer to Bribe*, 69 A.L.R.2d 1397 (1960).

Davis, R. P., *Entrapment to Commit Offense with respect to Gambling or Lotteries*, 31 A.L.R.2d 1212 (1953).

Derrick, John H., *Burden of Proof as to Entrapment Defense—State Cases*, 52 A.L.R.4th 775 (1987).

Entrapment as Defense to Charge of Selling or Supplying Narcotics where Government Agents Supplied Narcotics to Defendant and Purchased Them from Him, 9 A.L.R.5th 464 (1975).

Feld, Daniel E., *Admissibility of Evidence of Other Offenses in Rebuttal of Defense of Entrapment*, 61 A.L.R.3d 293 (1975).

———, *Modern Status of the Law Concerning Entrapment to Commit Narcotics Offense—Federal Cases*, 22 A.L.R. FED. 731 (1975).

———, *Modern Status of the Law Concerning Entrapment to Commit Narcotics Offense—State Cases*, 62 A.L.R.3d 110 (1975).

Gascoyne, R. W., *Entrapment with Respect to Violation of Fish and Game Laws*, 75 A.L.R.2d 709 (1961).

Ghent, Jeffrey F., *Criminal Law: "Official Statement" Mistake of Law Defense*, 89 A.L.R.4th 1026 (1991).

Habeeb, Wade R., *Antagonistic Defenses as Ground for Separate Trials of Codefendants in Criminal Case*, 82 A.L.R.3d 245 (1978).

Instructing on Burden of Proof as to Defense of Entrapment in Federal Criminal Case, 28 A.L.R. FED. 767 (1976).

Johnson, Sara L., *Entrapment to Commit Traffic Offense*, 34 A.L.R.4th 1167 (1984).

LeFevre, E., *Entrapment to Commit Offense against Laws Regulating Sales of Liquor,* 55 A.L.R.2d 1322 (1957).

Right of Criminal Defendant to Raise Entrapment Defense Based on Having Dealt with Other Party Who Was Entrapped, 15 A.L.R.5th 39 (1993).

Sarno, Gregory G., *Adequacy of Defense Counsel's Representation of Criminal Client Regarding Entrapment Defense,* 8 A.L.R.4th 1160 (1981).

———, *Entrapment Defense in Sex Offense Prosecutions,* 12 A.L.R.4th 413 (1982).

Schopler, E. H., *Accused's Right to, and Prosecution's Privilege against, Disclosure of Identity of Informant,* 76 A.L.R.2d 262 (1961).

Thomas, Tim A., *What Conduct of Federal Law Enforcement Authorities in Inducing or Cooperating in Criminal Offenses Raises Due Process Defense Distinct from Entrapment,* 97 A.L.R. FED. 273 (1990).

Travers, Timothy E., *Availability in Federal Court of Defense of Entrapment where Accused Denies Committing Acts which Constitute Offense Charged,* 54 A.L.R. FED. 644 (1981).

———, *Availability in State Court of Defense of Entrapment where Accused Denies Committing Acts which Constitute Offense Charged,* 5 A.L.R.4th 1128 (1981).

Veilleux, Danny R., *Actions by State Officials Involving Defendant as Constituting "Outrageous" Conduct Violating Due Process Guaranties,* 18 A.L.R.5th 1 (1994).

Ytreberg, D. E., *Larceny: Entrapment or Consent,* 10 A.L.R.3d 1121 (1966).

Zelin, Judy E., *Maintainability of Burglary Charge, where Entry into Building Is Made with Consent,* 58 A.L.R.4th 335 (1987).

Subject Index

Agents. *See* Government agents
Alcohol offenses, Ch. 1, § 2.1
Appeals, § 3.3(b)
Armed robbery, § 2.1, § 3.2(c)
Assaults, § 2.1, § 3.1(b)
Attempts, § 3.1(d), (e)

Breaking and entering, § 2.4(b), § 3.1(b)
Bribery, § 2.1
Burden of proof
  on entrapment, § 6.2
  jury instructions on, § 6.3(b)
  on want-of-element defenses,
    § 3.1(a), § 3.2(c)
Burglary, § 2.4(b), § 3.1(b)

Character
  evidence of, § 5.1(a), (d), § 5.2
  jury instructions on, § 6.3(b)
Codefendants, severance of, § 4.2
Conflicting defenses, § 4.3
Consent defense, § 3.1(b). *See also*
    Want-of-element defenses
Conspiracy, § 3.1(c), (e)
Contingent fees, § 2.3(c)
Corroborating evidence, § 5.1(c)
Criminal convictions, § 5.1(b), (d).
    See also Prior bad acts

Derivative entrapment, § 2.4(c)

Diminished capacity, § 6.2(b), § 6.3(b)
Dismissal. *See* Nonsuit; Pretrial
    dismissal
Driving while impaired, § 2.1
Drug offenses
  attempt, § 3.1(e)
  conspiracy, § 3.1(e)
  defenses
    entrapment, § 2.1
    outrageous conduct, § 3.3(a)
    public authority, § 3.2(b)
    sentencing entrapment, § 3.4
    want-of-element, § 3.1(e)
Due Process
  disclosure of identity of
    informant, § 4.1
  entrapment by estoppel, § 3.2(a)
  inconsistent defenses, § 4.3(d)
  outrageous conduct defense, § 3.3
  sentencing entrapment, § 3.4
Duress defense, § 2.4(a), § 5.4

Entrapment by estoppel, § 3.2(a)
Expert testimony, § 5.4
Explosives offenses, § 2.1, § 3.3(a)

Fish and game violations, § 2.1
Full-circle transactions, § 2.1, § 2.3(c)

Gambling, § 2.1

Government agents
  generally, § 2.4
  jury instructions on, § 6.3(b)
Guilty pleas, § 3.3(b)

Hearsay
  conversations with government
    agents, § 5.3
  about prior bad acts, § 5.1(c)
  reasonable suspicion, § 2.5(b),
    § 5.1(c)
  reputation, § 5.2

Impeachment, § 5.1(a), (b)
Impossibility defense, § 3.1(d), (e)
Inconsistent defenses, § 4.3
Inducement
  burden of proving, § 6.2
  and entrapment by estoppel,
    § 3.2(a)
  jury instructions on, § 6.3(b)
  meaning of, § 2.2, § 2.3
Ineffective assistance of counsel, Ch. 1
Informants
  disclosure of identity of, § 4.1
  inducement by, § 2.3(c), § 2.4(b)
  jury instructions on, § 6.3(b)
Innocent intent defense, § 3.2(c)
Insanity defense, § 6.1
Instructions. See Jury instructions
Intermediaries, unwitting, § 2.4(c)

Jury instructions
  burden to obtain, § 6.2(b)
  giving of, § 6.3(a)
  wording of, § 6.3(b)

Larceny, § 2.1, § 3.1(b)

Mental state. See Predisposition
Mitigating factors, § 2.1, § 3.4
Murder, § 3.1(b), (d)

Necessity defense, § 2.4(a)
Nonsuit, § 6.2(c)

Objective test, § 2.2
Obscenity offenses, § 2.1
Opinion testimony, § 5.2
Outrageous conduct defense, § 3.3.
  See also Due Process

Pattern jury instructions, § 6.3(b)
Perjury, § 2.1
Pleading requirements, § 6.1
Positional predisposition, § 2.5(b)
Possession of stolen goods, § 2.1,
  § 3.1(d)
Predisposition
  burden of proving, § 6.2
  and consent defense, § 3.1(b)
  jury instructions on, § 6.3(b)
  meaning of, Ch. 1, § 2.2, § 2.5
  and outrageous conduct defense,
    § 3.3(a)
Pretrial dismissal, § 2.1, § 3.3(b)
Prior bad acts
  admissibility of, § 2.2, § 2.5(b),
    § 5.1
  prior good acts compared,
    § 5.1(d)
Prostitution, § 2.1
Public authority defense, § 3.2(b)

Reasonable suspicion, § 2.5(b),
  § 5.1(c)
Receiving stolen goods, § 2.1, § 3.1(d)
Reliance defenses, § 3.2
Reputation evidence, § 2.5(b), § 5.2
Robbery, § 2.1, § 3.2(c)

Self-defense, § 6.2(b), § 6.3(b)
Sentencing entrapment, § 3.4
Sentencing factors, § 2.1, § 3.4
Severance of codefendants, § 4.2
Sexual assaults, § 2.1, § 3.1(b)
Solicitation, § 3.1(c)
Standing, § 2.4(c)
State of mind. See Predisposition
Subjective test, § 2.2
Suppression of evidence, § 2.1

Theft offenses, § 2.1, § 3.1(b), (d)

Timing of government contact
  generally, § 2.5(c)
  jury instructions on, § 6.3(b)
  and prior bad acts, § 5.1(b)

Traffic offenses, § 2.1

Unwitting intermediaries, § 2.4(c)

Vicarious entrapment, § 2.4(c)

Violent offenses, § 2.1

Voluntary intoxication defense, § 6.2(b)

Want-of-element defenses
  and inconsistent defenses, § 4.3(b)
  types of, § 3.1, § 3.2(c)

Weapons offenses, § 2.1

Wildlife offenses. *See* Fish and game
  violations

Worthless checks, § 2.4(b)

www.ingramcontent.com/pod-product-compliance
Lightning Source LLC
Chambersburg PA
CBHW061833220326
41599CB00027B/5266